PLANT MAGIC at HOME

A COMPLETE GUIDE TO HARNESSING THE POWER OF NATURE FROM RITUALS TO DIYs

ENID BAXTER RYCE

Illustrated by
CLAIRE HARRUP

RUNNING PRESS
PHILADELPHIA

Note: This book is intended only as an informational guide for those wishing to know more about the subject matter of this book. It is not intended to replace the advice of a physician or qualified health provider or be a substitute for health-related advice. Neither the author nor the publisher shall be liable or responsible for any loss or damage allegedly arising from any information or suggestion in this book.

Text copyright © 2025 by Enid Baxter Ryce
Interior and cover illustrations copyright © 2025 by Claire Harrup
Cover copyright © 2025 by Hachette Book Group, Inc.

Hachette Book Group supports the right to free expression and the value of copyright. The purpose of copyright is to encourage writers and artists to produce the creative works that enrich our culture.

The scanning, uploading, and distribution of this book without permission is a theft of the author's intellectual property. If you would like permission to use material from the book (other than for review purposes), please contact permissions@hbgusa.com. Thank you for your support of the author's rights.

Running Press
Hachette Book Group
1290 Avenue of the Americas, New York, NY 10104
www.runningpress.com
@Running_Press

First Edition: July 2025

Published by Running Press, an imprint of Hachette Book Group, Inc.
The Running Press name and logo are trademarks of Hachette Book Group, Inc.

The Hachette Speakers Bureau provides a wide range of authors for speaking events. To find out more, go to www.hachettespeakersbureau.com or email HachetteSpeakers@hbgusa.com.

Running Press books may be purchased in bulk for business, educational, or promotional use. For more information, please contact your local bookseller or the Hachette Book Group Special Markets Department at Special.Markets@hbgusa.com.

The publisher is not responsible for websites (or their content) that are not owned by the publisher.

Print book cover and interior design by Susan Van Horn

Library of Congress Cataloging-in-Publication Data
Names: Ryce, Enid Baxter, author. | Harrup, Claire, illustrator.
Title: Plant magic at home : a complete guide to harnessing the power of nature from rituals to DIYs / Enid Baxter Ryce ; illustrated by Claire Harrup.
Description: First edition. | Philadelphia : Running Press, 2025. | Includes bibliographical references and index.
Identifiers: LCCN 2024041405 (print) | LCCN 2024041406 (ebook) | ISBN 9780762488896 (hardcover) | ISBN 9780762488902 (ebook)
Subjects: LCSH: Human-plant relationships. | Plants—Therapeutic use. | Well-being.
Classification: LCC QK46.5.H85 R93 2025 (print) | LCC QK46.5.H85 (ebook) | DDC 581.6/3—dc23/eng/20241119
LC record available at https://lccn.loc.gov/2024041405
LC ebook record available at https://lccn.loc.gov/2024041406

ISBNs: 978-0-7624-8889-6 (hardcover), 978-0-7624-8890-2 (ebook)

Printed in China

TLF

10 9 8 7 6 5 4 3 2 1

For my family,

homegrown and foraged.

CONTENTS

Introduction: The Fifth Direction .... *vii*

PART ONE: GATHER 1
Foraging for Magical Plants 2
Magical Gardens 9

PART TWO: HARVEST 39
Flower Grimoire 40
Trees, Herbs, and Roots Grimoire 67
Kitchen Grimoire 95

PART THREE: REAP 121
Harnessing the Elements to Extract Plant Color 122
Making Inks and Paints 135
Color Magic 155
Seasonal Calendar of Natural Arts Projects 166
Creating Your Own Grimoire 174

CONCLUSION: A BENEDICTION OF RUNES 188

Bibliography *193*
Acknowledgments *197*
Index *198*
About the Author *204*

INTRODUCTION: THE FIFTH DIRECTION

As you move through the world, whether you are in the wilderness, city, or suburbs, you'll encounter plants. Bougainvillea vines etch themselves over brick walls. Dandelions squeeze through sidewalk cracks. Gingko trees rooted in cement squares wave their ancient fans as you pass. Sometimes, we may be oblivious to them as we rush through the world with our devices. But they are always here for us.

Plants may draw you in with their healing and nourishing properties, interconnectedness, and beauty. Perhaps you sense their magical potential, pausing to wonder at the language they speak most loudly: color.

How do you engage with these beings that sustain us? This book illuminates a path to connecting with plants and their meanings, histories, and healing and culinary properties. You will explore recipes and spells from texts spanning more than 2,000 years and learn simple processes to make inks, paints, and other handmade botanical crafts. You will learn to cultivate pigment gardens and sustainably forage for powerful plants.

When we explore the magic connected to nature's beauty and mystery, we may sense that we are remembering something we once knew. As we begin this practice, let your memories of color, nature, and the elements resurface. As children, we felt nature's powers coursing through us. We cultivated our relationship with Mother Nature—one of giving and receiving. Let the petals, leaves, and roots reconnect you to the world and yourself.

What do you remember?

I remember the saturated colors of the fire's embers—the only source of heat in the house, even as long icicles caught the winter light outside the window's old, uneven glass. Our well water, so polluted that we had to keep our mouths closed in the shower, was often stained red by the shale dust it ran through. I remember staining my mother's yarns with pigments derived primarily from plants.

Goldenrod transformed into green dyes, deep purple pokeberries to red, and pine gave way to brown. Each yarn threaded through the loom that towered in her bedroom. Plants had always been especially magical for her. She knew them as inherently transformative—and not only in their pigmentation. Her plants were also for nourishment and healing.

Next to the big vegetable area where most of our food grew was a medicinal garden surrounded by old, weathered bricks. I liked to sit on them, gazing at the tiny forests of moss that crept toward the fragrant, precious herbs they protected. Companion plants grew strategically to support the garden. We could harvest them from the garden and the surrounding forest for healing, spells, or color. Often, it was a combination of all three.

I thought my family practiced old-fashioned knowing, and it felt magical. But I recently realized how much of what we did was a mix of ancient and contemporary Green Magic—magic connected to the natural world. I find the echoes of my mother's magical gardens and the colors that wove through her loom in my experiences with plants today.

Where did it come from? Ireland, Scotland, the Sephardim, or our Salem witch forebearers? The many indigenous and diasporic ancestors that make up our family? Sometimes, all we have are the traces—woven strands of family recipes, incantations, healing practices, and other ways of knowing. They connect us to the magic that courses through all the dimensions of nature—including us. We are part of nature. When we feel the link to the unseen, we are hyperaware of the mysteries hidden in swaying leaves and twisted tree trunks.

Every landscape has secrets that it whispers in many languages. Color is a powerful tool that nature uses to communicate. From the bright hues of poisonous snakes to the muted pastels of purifying sages, colors remind us of elemental truths we inherently understand. We can reconnect to our innate magical being when we focus on color. Red fills you with passion, and orange is creativity. Yellow connects you to the fierce power of your purpose. Green heals your heart. Blue encourages you to speak your truth. Indigo and purple are spirit colors: support from the unseen world.

These days, I live in California. Walking in the wilderness here, one might hear the sudden distant roar of thousands of tiny tree frogs or meander through a grove of chaparral oak trees draped with soft sea green lichen and emerge to find a deep, hidden pool of water so still that it perfectly reflects the sky—a vernal pool.

By summertime, such small and ephemeral bodies of water will have disappeared—their dry beds baking in the sun.

I love to take my children to wander in the forest. Once, we walked over dry, cracked clay. Soon enough, they were protesting. (They have to be tricked or bribed into hiking. Even then, they do it grumpily.) We were creeping carefully toward the dry bed of a vernal pool. Most people don't know these gentle, isolated lakes in the forest are home to families of ducks, endangered salamanders, and elegant, long-legged bugs.

It was vibrant.

The empty lake bed was full of dry, tall, reddish stalks peppered with tiny round husks. We checked out the plant identifier app: wild barley. It's invasive to the region, so removing some might be helpful.

"Should we try it?" the older kid asked.

My younger son agreed, and they began collecting stalks, shaking the husks into our cloth bag. Enough to boil into a bath and see what color emerged.

We stopped for a snack. One of the plums had turned. My son suggested we try making color from it, too.

On the way home, we stopped to collect the last acorn shells left on the branches by deer and squirrels who had taken the nuts. The shells make brown or silver ink. And we found light tan oak galls that make black ink. My *Hamilton*-obsessed teen loved the idea that Alexander had used the same ink centuries ago.

From that day, we still have small jars of color, test swatches, and oak gall samples saved for more color-making.

We collect these plants and their colors as focal points for meditation, spell recipes, art and craft supplies, and medicines. They also serve as journals of our adventures.

When my children have trouble sleeping, we do a color meditation spell, imagining we breathe specific hues into our bodies. Thinking of plants and their fruits and flowers helps us to see the colors as we inhale. (See page 164.) And, with each color, I hope they have memories of finding or growing plants that speak through it.

The process of creating plant color magic is simultaneously exciting and relaxing. It supports human and environmental health. And it reconnects us to nature's magic through the language we share with the trees, the flowers, and the sky: the language of color.

One way color speaks is through its connection to the elements. Fire is red, orange, and yellow. Water is blue. These colors express the inherent properties of each element: hot or cool. In magical expression, the symbol of the pentagram can signify the elements: fire, air, water, earth, and the fifth one of spirit. Including spirit as an element recognizes the existence of another invisible, celestial force that moves us and all of nature. Many ancient cultures recognized a fifth direction. Centuries ago, maps might've included north, south, east, west, and a direction that connects the depths of the earth to the heavens.

Plants embody that fifth direction. Their roots reach deep into the ground, and they simultaneously stretch up, connecting to the sky. They are nourished by air, sunlight, soil, and water—all the elements. Natural magic practice recognizes that plants relate to the fifth element. This magic, used by ancient people worldwide for spiritual and healing practices, is still available to us today.

*In this book, we will travel
in the fifth direction.
Through this exploration,
I hope you find a creative
and fun way to connect with
nature, spirit, and your
childhood sense of wonder.*

Part One
GATHER

In the E. E. Cummings poem "maggie and milly and molly and may," the characters go to the beach and collect objects. May finds a "smooth round stone, as small as a world and as large as alone." The poem's last line is "It's always ourselves we find in the sea."

As we move through nature gathering plants, whether foraging or harvesting, we also gather insights and become more attuned to patterns and changes in the world. What we notice in the landscape reflects what is happening within us.

In nature, we gather ourselves.

FORAGING FOR MAGICAL PLANTS

The Art of Scrying

When I am teaching, I start every class by taking my students outside to do some kind of perceptual experiment. Once, because I asked them to, my students squinted up at a complicated sky. It was a weak winter blue. The wisps of cirrus clouds suggested a cold rain was about a day away. The sun was climbing, bright and unobstructed, but a haze blurred the horizon, creeping off the ocean and into the valley. Soon, we would be engulfed in fog.

"What do you see?" I asked. I'd just taught them to shade their eyes with their palms—a trick taught in Victorian times when the landed gentry were formally instructed in *visual acuity*—the skill of distinguishing shapes in the landscape.

My students stood silently, obediently, looking up, until one, braver than the rest, finally said, "Nothing."

A few others laughed.

"Nothing?!" I couldn't believe it. "Do you all see nothing?"

They agreed. They saw nothing.

After pausing to push away the fear that I was hallucinating, I pointed to what I saw. The gathering haze. The wisps.

"Oh yeah," one said. "I see that now."

The rest of them nodded.

I sighed with relief.

In the ancient world, my looking up at the sky and telling you that it would be foggy later and rain tomorrow would be seen as a form of fortune-telling. I would have been *scrying* the sky. There are many scrying methods—gazing into crystal balls, at tea leaves, flames, and bowls of water—to predict what is to come.

The origin of this word *scry* is probably *descry*: another term from the 1200s meaning "to see, discern," that is perhaps from Old French *descrier*, "publish, proclaim, announce," and related to the Latin *describere*, "to write down, copy" (like *describe*). From the mid-fourteenth century, *scry* is defined as "detect, find out, discover" (something concealed), also "discover by vision, get sight of."

Scrying or predicting the future requires the ability to discern signs and describe their meaning. It wasn't that my students couldn't physically see the clouds and the haze; it was that they couldn't discern anything significant from them. They could not distinguish the clouds' shapes or interpret their meaning, because they aren't used to looking up at the sky.

Our inability to read nature is a characteristic of modern life. Some botanists talk about *tree blindness*—the common inability to recognize species of trees. Long ago, people used to know the trees' names immediately. They knew which would burn or grow back fast or provide shelter, medicine, or food. Scrying meant surviving.

Scrying for Foraging: Respecting Our Home

Foraging for plants allows us to relearn how to scry the trees, the sky, and all of nature. We need to predict which plants we need and discern which ones we should not remove, lest we damage the ecosystem. That word *ecosystem* comes from the Greek root *oikos*, meaning "home." The nature we walk through is our home.

For this reason, I recommend not disturbing the mosses, lichens, or biological crusts.

Moss

These ancient, rootless, nonflowering plants are essential in caring for the other plants and the tiny, delicate animals around them. They keep the soil moist so that the rest can thrive, regulate the soil temperature, and exponentially increase the diversity of plant communities. I encourage you not to collect or disturb them. Perhaps instead, lie on the ground and stare at mosses, discerning their complicated, lush environments. Imagine what it would be like to be tiny and walk through them.

Lichen

Lichens are not plants. They are a combination of fungus and algae that take a long time to grow. Where I live, lichens function in symbiosis with chaparral oaks, a rare species threatened by climate change. The lichen hangs long, cool green, and dreamy from the oak branches, increasing the tree's ability to photosynthesize—to eat light. Lichens do not compete with the trees. They draw all their nourishment from what floats microscopically in the air.

Biological Crusts

Biological crusts don't look like much. They may resemble dried-out moss, black bumps, or a subtle ground cover. But once you get close, you might find an almost invisible grove of hundreds of mushrooms, each the size of a pinhead. These crusts occur mainly in drier landscapes, where the earth rarely freezes. They are made of mosses, fungi, and bacteria that help the soil thrive and plants grow while keeping carbon out of the atmosphere. The most sensitive crusts can take thousands of years to recover when disturbed.

WHEN IN DOUBT: Just as we can be dangerous for plants, plants can do harm to our bodies. This book is not offering professional medical guidance. Some people are more at risk of harm from certain plants than others. Please exercise caution when working with plants. Don't pick up plants you are not fully certain are safe.

Helpful Disturbance

If we harvest invasive plants, that's a helpful disturbance. My community is constantly battling the fast-growing ice plant. While it's beautiful and makes sense in its home environment of coastal South Africa, in Coastal California it displaces native grasses that expertly hold the loose topsoil with long, winding roots. The local animals depend on the grasses' soft, tall, green and gold blades and the bugs that shelter in them. Wherever there's ice plant, there are no grasses. That's what makes invasive plants disruptive to ecosystems, to our homes.

How can you tell if a plant is invasive? First, identify it using a plant app or book. Then, check its scientific or common name on the USDA plant database. It will tell you if the plant is harmful or protected.

Why Forage?

We forage to collect plants to create arts and crafts, spells, pigments, gardens, or meals. Rather than planting and nurturing seeds in a slow-moving gardening process, we can quickly collect what we need—for free. What we are cultivating as we forage is a sense of place. We learn the natural rhythms of a landscape, scry its hidden messages, and heal ourselves by being outside and moving. All of this benefits our physical, mental, and emotional well-being.

Foragers are often not just collectors; we are environmental stewards. We thin and remove competition, sustaining the plants we collect from. We leave the place cleaner than we found it. We advocate for protecting the natural spaces we cherish, living in reciprocity with the plants we love.

When gathered, the plants featured in this book will provide magic, nourishment, and beautiful colors.

Foraging Basics

WHAT TO BRING:

- Weather-appropriate clothing and footwear
- Sun protection
- Bug repellent
- Gloves
- A big bag (I like backpacks)
- Little bags, jars, or boxes to store little things
- Marker for labeling
- Scissors or clippers
- Plant identifier (app or book)
- USDA plant database—for a plant's status (requiring protection or invasive)
- A small first-aid kit
- Water and snacks
- An offering of thanks, like coffee grounds (beloved by all plants)

Where to Forage

It's always a good idea to first check if it's OK to be somewhere collecting plants. For example, foraging and collecting in national parks, state parks, and BLM lands is prohibited, while national forests may allow collecting for personal use.

Foraging doesn't have to happen in pristine wilderness. Collect plants that grow between sidewalk squares, at the edges of empty lots, and along abandoned train tracks. You can also collect plants from weed piles and invasive plant removal sites and after community events when flowers or decorative squash are discarded.

Foraging Technique

When harvesting pieces of a living plant, experts recommend taking only 10 percent of a plant (one leaf for every ten) and no more than 20 percent (two leaves for every ten). This will ensure that the plant will continue to live.

When collecting seeds and acorns, applying this ratio will ensure the continuation of the plant's family, as it feeds families of local animals.

When taking pieces of a plant, first check to see where new growth and buds are emerging. Avoid cutting below the buds so that the plant can bloom again. Using scissors lessens the disturbance.

Before you leave, you can give an offering—like a pinch of coffee grounds, sprinkled at the base of the plant, which they love.

Remember to Take in the Beauty

As you forage, take time to discern, or scry, your surroundings. Look at the forms the land takes in hillsides and valleys, the communities of trees, and the overhead paths of birds. Listen for the footsteps of animals, big and small, and the songs of bugs, hums of bees, and cries of hawks.

Whether in the wilderness or cities, we are in nature.
All our senses help us to scry.

Meditative Walking Spell

As you move over the ground, pay attention to its unevenness, softness, and hardness. The ground is supporting you.

Breathe deeply into your belly. Stop now and then, and close your eyes. Inhale and exhale five times.

Take in the scents, sounds, and movement of the air.

When ready, open your eyes.

What do you discern?

As you walk, let your arms be loose and swing, releasing your shoulders.

Set the intention:

I am part of nature. I cherish my relationships with the earth, sea, and sky inhabitants. I am grateful for the world's abundance. Nature's beauty reminds me that I am loved.

Foraging Spell

Focus on the plant you are interested in harvesting. Notice its unique leaves, many tones, and texture. Notice its movement and its relationship with its neighbors.

When we whisper in the old language
We make sounds of wonder
in tones of gratitude.
When we whisper in the old language,
we understand each other.
I carry you with me.

Whisper:
May I learn what you need me to know.

MAGICAL GARDENS

I remember my father carrying me through the garden on a moonless night. I was small and had awoken, struggling to breathe.

It's croup, the doctor told my mother on the phone. *She needs humidity.*

First, they'd rushed me into the bathroom and turned the shower on hot, encouraging me to try to inhale the steam. But soon, the water ran reddish-brown, tinted with slate dust from our well's bottom. My parents had to turn off the shower so the well wouldn't run dry. They had two other children to mix powdered milk for in the morning.

So my father scooped me up and carried me out into the darkness of my mother's moon garden. I knew there were flowers out there that only bloomed at night, but I had never seen them. Over his shoulder, I strained to get a look at their ghostly white and shadowed purple forms.

My mother's moon garden was at the forest's edge—the moonflowers creeping over the feet of the trees. Their scents were heavier than those of daytime plants in order to help pollinators find them in the dark. Evening primroses called to fluttering moths. Jasmine hosted herds of beetles. Their blooms' shapes echoed the stars, bright in the moonless sky. All over the Western Hemisphere, the night pollinators were working. South of us, plants like cacti, mangoes, and bananas called to pollinating bats. Yucca plants communed with yucca moths. I was in the swaying shadows of a garden's secret life.

At night, cooler temperatures allow humidity to rise. Plants focus on respiration, and their leaves release moisture. Thanks to the garden and the forest, it was easier for me to breathe.

My body relaxed, and I slipped slowly to sleep.

A Moon Garden

There are certain plants that open in the night, their heavy scents beckoning the less visual pollinators who operate under the moon. During the day, a moon garden will appear lush and green. Some plants might never be suspected of having more to offer than their lovely leaves. They protect their delicate, pale blossoms from the sun's rays, only unfurling for the bats, moths, and beetles who might visit them once the earth cools. Select a corner of your garden that will open with secret night blooms while most everyone is asleep. Place it near your bedroom window, so you can sense when the flowers awaken.

Plants for a Moon Garden

Angel's trumpet *(Brugmansia)*

Chocolate daisy *(Berlandiera lyrata)*

Evening primrose *(Oenothera biennis)*

Evening rain lily *(Zephyranthes drummondii)*

Flowering tobacco *(Nicotiana alata)*

Foamflower *(Tiarella cordifolia)*

Four o'clocks *(Mirabilis jalapa)*

Gardenia *(Gardenia jasminoides)*

Lily 'Casa Blanca' *(Lillium)*

Mock orange *(Philadelphus coronarius)*

Moonflower *(Ipomoea alba)*

Night-blooming jasmine *(Cestrum nocturnum)*

Night phlox *(Zaluzianskya ovata)*

Night-scented stock *(Matthiola longipetala)*

Queen of the night *(Epiphyllum oxypetalum)*

A Dream Garden

If my father had carried me over to his cacti, it might have been even easier for me to breathe that night. One of the ways that desert plants like succulents and cacti preserve moisture is by holding their breath during the day. At night, they open their stomata (the tiny mouths on the undersides of leaves—or on the body or stem of cacti), releasing oxygen. Moisture escapes with their exhalation, but less than would during the day.

Plants for a Dream Garden

Areca palm *(Dypsis lutescens)*

Snake plant *(Dracaena trifasciata)*

Money (jade) plant *(Crassula ovata)*

Aloe vera *(Aloe vera)*

Peace lily *(Spathiphyllum)*

Our ancestors believed that time is a circle, and that is how we experience time in dreams. What we see is simultaneously a lesson from the past and a prophecy. Having these plants in your bedroom or outside the window is wonderful for air quality as you sleep, improving your sleeping intuition. They are the dream plants.

Dream Spell

To be whispered before sleep with a night plant in the form of dried herbs, fresh leaves, or crushed blossoms under your pillow; drawn or photographic images of the plant; a plant's scent sprayed on the pillow, on the skin, or wafting through the air; or lovingly picturing a night plant in your mind:

Under the moon's wax and wane,
I am made of dust from ancient stars
whose children dance
sparkling in the darkness.
I close my eyes,
My dreams shimmer, woven from mystery.
May they show me my path
May I awaken to my purpose.
Thank you, Night.

Repeat:

May I be guided by the part of me
that connects me to the Mystery.

Gardening by the Moon

Since ancient times, gardeners have looked to the moon for guidance on when, what, and how to plant. Just as the moon pulls on the seas to create the tides, gardens may shift with the moon's effect on water in the soil. Just as the sun's light impacts plant growth, so may the moon's. The ancients believed the moon's phases also influenced our creative flow.

MOON PHASE GARDENING

MOON PHASE	MEANING	IN THE GARDEN
New moon	**New Beginnings.** Time for a reset. Rest and gather energy.	Plant annual flowers, fruit, and vegetables that bear crops aboveground (e.g., tomatoes, corn, beans, vines, and marigolds).
Waxing crescent moon	**Intentions.** Set intentions by visualizing specific outcomes for the coming cycle. Listen to your intuition.	Plant blackberries, raspberries, and caned plants.
First quarter moon	**Action.** Create a to-do list. Accomplish first steps.	Weed plants and thin shoots.
Waxing gibbous moon	**Recover from Setbacks.** Assess and recalibrate your plan.	Best time for planting during drought conditions. Harvest blackberries to break all curses.
Full moon	**Harvest, Fruition.** Your attention to your intentions produced results. Charge your magical objects by placing them under the full moon overnight. Leave a jar of water outside to make moon water for spells.	Harvest spicy root vegetables like horseradish and ginger. Plant lettuces. Weed. Transplant seedlings and succulent cuttings.
Waning gibbous moon	**Introspection.** What feels right? How should you adjust your approach or recalibrate your goals?	Plant root crops and those that produce food belowground, (e.g., onions, potatoes, and carrots). Plant perennials, biennials, and flowering bulbs, roots, and tubers. Harvest aboveground produce, herbs, and flowers.

continued

MOON PHASE GARDENING *continued*

MOON PHASE	MEANING	IN THE GARDEN
Third quarter moon	**Detach.** Reconnect with love and gratitude. Let go of your expectations. The outcomes will surprise you.	Plant strawberries. Divide plants.
Waning crescent moon	**Reflection.** What have you learned through this moon cycle? How have you grown?	Complete harvest and plant cover crop.
Back to the new moon	**New Beginning.** The cycle resets, but it is a spiral. Because you have grown from your recent experiences, you begin in a new place.	Plant annual flowers, fruit, and vegetables that bear crops aboveground (e.g., tomatoes, corn, beans, vines, and marigolds).

Understanding the Shadows in Our Moon Gardens

My mother planted a moon garden to call to the Celtic spirits that rule the night: Rhiannon, goddess of the moon. Aine, the queen of fairies. Caer Ibormeith, the goddess of sleep and dreams. All goddesses to help her avoid the dreaded banshees, the followers of Morrigan—wild, screaming wraiths who could turn up outside the window, terrifying me.

Who do you wish to call? Lailah, the Hebrew angel of the night, to support creativity and conception? Artemis or Diana, goddess of the moon and hunt, to bolster your independence? Nyx and Erebus, the powerful couple ruling night and darkness? Kek, hailing from ancient Egypt? Ratri, Chandra, Rahu; Nut, Shalim, Metztli; Goddess Mawu, creator of all, goddess of the moon—all these nighttime deities can aid, inspire, and protect us. Their symbols are often nighttime pollinator animals—moths, bats, owls, and beetles. Sometimes feared across cultures, they are recognized as beings that carry messages of transformation.

Plant a night garden to call on the help you need to understand your shadows. Through this transformation, you will grow into yourself and the fullness of your story.

Hecate's Garden

Hecate is the goddess of liminal spaces: boundaries, night and day, forest and meadow, what you know and don't know. She is the goddess of what is in-between. This is where intuition lives. To understand what transformational energies you need, visit the garden of Hecate. To do this, spend time walking in nature or gardens. Note what plants have called to you. When you learn their meanings, you will strengthen your intuition and communication with the Otherworld.

The plants that call to you, the plants you seek out, and the plants that appear in your dreams are *your* garden of Hecate, growing wild and wonderful in the middle of the forests of your spirit.

Spell for Shadows

Shadows are only scary and shameful
if I keep silent.
When I talk about what frightens me,
I am free.
Thank you, shadows.
I will speak of you.

Repeat:
Shame and fear
don't cast your shadows here.
Whatever frightens me,
I speak of and am free.

Repeat the last lines as a mantra for seven days. Keep a journal of what comes to mind. Choose a trusted friend or counselor to share your shadows with.

Daytime Gardens

A Magical Healing Garden

These powerful, magical plants can be placed in full sun. They will bloom at different times and thrive at different temperatures. They can also be grown in containers inside, on a window, or outside an apartment.

MAGIC HEALING PLANT	NATURAL POWER
Arnica	Pain relief
Basil	Banishment
Borage	Merriment
Chamomile	Relaxation
Holy basil	Healing
Lavender	Calming
Mint	Cooling
Mugwort	Healing
Poppy	Dreams
Rosemary	Memory
Sage	Cleansing
Saint-John's-wort	Happiness
Vervain	Joy
Yarrow	Intuition

Spell for Light

Gentle Light surrounds me.
Gentle Light within me.
Light falls on flowers.
Colors lift me into joy.
Thank you, light.

Repeat:
To be happy feels right,
So shines my light.

Repeat the last lines as a mantra for seven days.

MAKE A SPELL CLOTH

Use beautiful, powerful plants to create textiles resembling botanical samplers. Invite your friends to pick which plants they are drawn to or which powers they want in their home. By printing with these plants, you create a magic spell, calling in these properties to support those who carry them or keep them in their home.

To extract color from all the plants listed for the Magical Healing Garden—or any others that might speak to you on your foraging expeditions or from lists later in this book—I recommend using the hapa zome technique on light-colored, washed cotton. (See page 123.) For a more intense color, soak the cotton in soy milk and let it dry.

Each plant will respond to this process differently. With practice, you will become more skilled at hammering different kinds of plants. Before starting a spell cloth, create a few tests.

1. *Select a leaf and lay it veiny side up. Lay another of the same species smooth side up. Begin hammering lightly at the center of each leaf, circling out to edges. If there is not a vivid impression, increase the force. Notice which side of the leaf you prefer.*

2. *To test flowers, begin at the center, lightly. Do you like the color the center yields? If not, move on to the petals. Do they need a great deal of force applied to print? Or will that create splashes? This depends on the moisture each plant contains as you work with it. Be sure to hammer to the edges of each petal.*

These tests will help you plan your spell cloth.

An example spell cloth: For a friend experiencing anxiety, arrange lavender and borage blossoms and sprigs of sage, mint, and vervain leaves over half a white cotton cloth. Lay the other half gently over this arrangement, being careful not to disturb the design. Crush the flowers and leaves by hammering on the cotton. It will smell wonderful!

Once you're sure you have hammered over all the surfaces, separate the cotton and let it dry somewhere warm. When the plant matter has dried, brush it off, and you'll have a beautiful, scented spell cloth for your friend.

Magical Rainbow Pigment Garden

To create a garden focused on color magic, plant pigment plants. These plants have been cultivated for thousands of years to produce the most vivid, permanent colors. They are easy to care for and thrive in full sun. Check to see whether, when, and how they flourish in your climate.

For passion	**Red:** Beet, madder (root), pokeberry, red Hopi amaranth
For creativity	**Orange:** Coreopsis, madder (root), marigold, rhubarb (root), sumac
For intuition	**Yellow:** Dyer's chamomile, fennel, goldenrod, marigold, onion
For interconnectedness	**Green:** Dandelion, dark purple dahlia (petals, leaves, and stems), dyer's chamomile (leaves and stems), nettle
For communication	**Blue:** Black bean, hollyhock, Japanese indigo,* red cabbage, woad*
For the mystical	**Indigo:** Black bean, Japanese indigo*
For psychic power	**Purple:** Cosmos, elderberry, fox grape, Hopi sunflower, morning glory
For grounding	**Brown:** Anise, avocado, sage, zinnia

Please see the notes on these plants' pages in part two. They are considered invasive in some places. You can grow invasive species enclosed in planting bags, or don't allow them to go to seed by harvesting the blossoms early.

Pollinator Gardens

An ecosystem without humans might thrive, but without pollinators, it would collapse. Pollinators include bats, bees, beetles, birds, butterflies, flies, and moths. And they communicate in nature's languages of color, movement, and scent. To attract specific animals, consider plants of their favorite color.

POLLINATOR	COLOR PREFERENCE	ENERGIES
Bats	Night-blooming green, white, and purple	Love, healing, psychic senses
Bees	Bright white, yellow, blue, and UV light	Cleansing, intuition, communication, the Otherworld
Beetles	White and green	Healing, love
Birds	Red, purple, orange, and white	Lust, psychic senses, creativity, healing
Butterflies	All bright colors, especially red and purple	The spectrum of life and mystery
Flies	Pale colors, brown, dark purple, and spotted surfaces	The Underworld
Moths	Night-blooming dull red, purple, pink, and white	Passion, psychic insight, transformation, healing

Important carriers of magic and wisdom, pollinators also facilitate most plants' reproduction. Many of them are predators who feed on garden pests. With the loss of wildlands, the impacts of pesticides, and many gardeners preferring to keep plants from going to seed, the pollinator popula-

tion is struggling. They need wild, pollen-rich habitats that provide shelter for nests, hydration, and safe resting places.

To create a pollination garden, plant large clusters of plants that grow well in your climate. Larger clusters will offer more places to hide and breed. Add a natural sheltering feature, like a decomposing log. To encourage nesting, allow plants to grow wild.

Skip the pesticides and mulch. If ground cover is necessary, use dry leaves. Add a water feature or a place where water can puddle for drinking.

Allow your flowers to be messy and complete their life cycle. They will soon contain the seeds for your next season's garden. Leave their dead leaves and stems long as nesting spaces. Don't disturb cocoons and chrysalises. Look out for tiny hummingbird nests and give them space.

Consider combinations of beloved plants that are good for your climate and bring helpful energies to your home. Each planting zone has pollination garden guides through the USDA and similar agencies.

Examples include:

Bee balm	Protection, psychic clarity
Columbine	Trembling with passion
Cosmos	Harmony
Crimson clover	Giving everything
Lavender	Calm
Milkweeds*	Remembrance, dignity, and freedom
Nasturtiums	Victory
Rosemary	Remembrance
Sage	Cleansing
Sunflowers	Wishes and beautiful surroundings
Zinnias	Endurance

*Beloved by monarch butterflies, different species are best in different planting zones.

Companion Planting

My mother always planted her tomatoes with marigolds.

When I asked her why, she said simply, "For protection."

Later, conversing with a botanist, I learned my mother was right. I found out that not only do marigolds' strong scent repel some tomato-eating pests, but their roots also entwine with the tomatoes' roots and protect them from troublesome, wormlike, microscopic pests called nematodes. My mother, who had not been formally educated in botany or microbiology, learned this from my grandmother, who has barely gone to school at all. Whenever I plant marigolds, I wonder, "How did they know?"

It's a garden mystery.

I recommend wild and messy gardens, not only because they are spellbinding but because they tap into nature's magic of interconnectedness. This magic can be harnessed intentionally with the ancient practice of companion planting. The Three Sisters or Milpa is a beautiful example of this from North America. Many indigenous cultures traditionally place three plants together: corn, squash, and beans. The corn grows tall. The beans climb the corn. The beans pull nitrogen from the air and, underground, work hard to transform it into food for the other plants. The squash needs lots of nitrogen to become rich in nutrients. It spreads its spiky leaves over the ground, protecting the three plants from weeds, rodents, and other pests. The broad leaves keep the soil cool and moist.

Corn is full of starchy carbs. Beans have lots of protein. Squash is full of vitamins. When we eat these three together, they are a balanced and healthy meal. We nourish our plants, and they nourish us. Maybe we are the fourth sibling.

As Dr. Robin Wall Kimmerer writes in her book *Braiding Sweetgrass*:

Perhaps we should consider this a Four Sisters garden, for the planter is also an essential partner. It is she who turns up the soil, she who scares away the crows, and she who pushes seeds into the soil. . . . Corn, beans, and squash are fully domesticated; they rely on us to create the conditions under which they can grow.

When we engage in companion planting, we get more out of our garden's space, support our plants' and soils' health, and decrease the need for pesticides.

Some plants act as "trap crops" in the garden, creating a diversion that draws pests away from others, like tomatoes.

Other companion plants call to beneficial insects that will also prey on insect pests before they can damage your plants. These predatory insects include ladybugs, mantises, green lacewings, and parasitic wasps.

COMPANION COMBINATIONS

COMPANION	PLANT WITH	GARDEN POWER	POWERS
Basil	Tomatoes	Repels aphids and hornworms	Protection
Black-eyed peas	Tall flowers	Trap crop	Prosperity
Calendula	Pigment or healing garden	Pest repellent	Positivity
Catnip	Plant at garden borders.	Repels mice and Japanese beetles, mosquitoes, flies, mites	Courage
Chives	Herb garden	Pest repellent	Prosperity
Cilantro	Cabbage, cauliflower, kale, mustard Do not plant near carrots.	Repels aphids, Colorado potato beetles, spider mites Invites beneficial insects	Lust
Cosmos	Throughout garden	Attracts beneficial insects	Harmony
Dill	Squashes and vined fruits	Repels squash bugs	Lust, satisfaction
Marigold	Tomatoes	Trap crop and supports root health	Ancestors
Nasturtiums	Throughout garden	Repels pests, cools ground, and helps it retain moisture	Victory

COMPANION COMBINATIONS *continued*

COMPANION	PLANT WITH	GARDEN POWER	POWERS
Oregano	Cabbage, broccoli, and brussels sprouts	Repels cabbage moths	Happiness
Parsley	Herb garden	Attracts beneficial insects	Wisdom and travel
Radish	With root vegetables	Repellent and trap crop	Purification
Rosemary	Carrots, parsnips, and celery	Repels carrot rust flies and Mexican bean beetles	Memory
Thyme	Bell peppers	Repels spider mites and whiteflies	Luck and protection
Sage	Strawberries	Repels slugs	Cleansing
Zinnia	Near vegetables	Attracts beneficial insects	Endurance

Spell for Companionship

Speak this spell to a candle.
Visualize or offer a corn kernel,
a bean, and a squash flower.

*Vines weave and climb
To face the sun
Turning to the light,
we lift our branches.
I am nourished
nurtured
protected.
Under the soil,
we hold our root circle
gently
as our leaves shake
with laughter.*

Repeat:
*You are my tree,
your beauty, I see.
I am your tree,
nurtured and fully me.*

Soil Nourishing

Soils are communities of many beings working together to sustain life on earth. After the harvest is complete, planting cover crops can restore nutrients, supporting the soil's health and life.

Choose a cover crop that will thrive in your climate and plant it after the harvest during the waning crescent moon.

Asparagus	Passion
Basil	Protection and flying
Borage	Merriment
Broom corn	Purification and wind
Carrot	Fertility
Crimson clover	Giving everything
Garlic	Protection
Thyme	Luck and protection

Garden Design

My garden design process involves failure, foraging, scrying, and unlikely allies. I live at the edge of a national monument. It's gorgeous and teeming with wildlife—all wanting to destroy my garden. There are giant, clumsy wild turkeys; legions of snails; gangs of raccoons; little sweet voles that sucked entire olive tree saplings into the ground. But nothing crushed my dreams like the squirrels who descended upon my plants, decimating them.

I realized they would need 360-degree protection. Usually, this means beds with plastic covers, which soon disintegrate, harming the environment. After many failed experiments, I sewed cotton cheesecloth tightly around poles encircling my beds. The squirrels stopped noticing my garden.

All was well until an abandoned chicken showed up at my front door one evening. So we built a coop and got it a friend. I started tossing weeds into a big pile in the chicken run for them to snack on. Soon, a family of ground squirrels moved in under the pile. Feeling betrayed by my chickens, I watched the squirrels join them in munching on the weeds all morning. And, then, amazingly, those squirrels began to defend the space from all others. So now I have native plants, a pigment/dye garden, a magic and medicine garden, vegetables, pacifist chickens, and a family of squirrels running a protection racket. I give them weeds, and they patrol the gardens.

Because we need the plants and animals to work with us, creating a garden is like designing a planned community. Most experts recommend observing, starting small, and adding to your garden as you learn about the soil, light, and climate.

1. Scry the Garden Area

To garden in relationship with the landscape, the first step is to observe.

Where is it sunny?

Where is shade?

Where is partial shade?

Are there nearby conifers dropping needles that would inhibit growth?

Where is it moist?

Where is the soil rich?

Where is it sandy?

Be sure to observe at different times of day, remembering that the angles of the shade will change as the seasons do.

2. Mark the Area

Use sticks and string to identify what you've noticed, and start dividing your garden into sections.

3. Decide What Kind of Garden You'd Like

What type of garden or gardens would you like to grow? Magical, medicinal, floral, pigment, food, an urban window or balcony garden? Or a combination?

Select plants that will flourish throughout the year to keep your garden exciting. If this is your first garden, you may want to select plants described as "hearty," which means they are easy to keep healthy.

Here are some suggestions:

HEARTY PLANTS FOR SUN	HEARTY PLANTS FOR SHADE
Arnica	Asarum
Baby blue eyes	Astilbe
Daylily	Convallaria
Echinacea	Ferns
Geranium	Hosta
Heuchera	Liriope
Rudbeckia	Moss
Sedum	Nettle
Valerian	Primula

Most experts recommend starting with a combination of perennial plants (those that will keep coming back over the years) and annual plants (those that flourish for one season). This diversity will support soil health and keep the garden exciting throughout the year.

Below are a few hearty, long-flowering perennials that you can use to anchor your garden:

HEARTY, LONG-FLOWERING PERENNIALS	
'Moonshine' yarrow	Purple coneflower
Lesser calamint	Russian sage
Valerian*	'Goldsturm' black-eyed Susan
Tickseed	'Butterfly blue' scabiosa
Corydalis	'Stella de Oro' daylily

*Used to create Valium, valerian root matures in three years and can be employed as a powerful sleep aid. It may be harmful in combination with other drugs. An alternative is red valerian (Centranthus ruber).

4. Plan Your Garden

Now that you've chosen some plants, you are ready to create a plan. You can make a diagram, or if you're uncomfortable sketching, you can number each garden section and make notes and lists.

5. Measure

Roughly measure the dimensions of each area. This will help you understand how many of each species your area can hold.

6. Research

What planting zone are you in?

What are your zone's early, late, and long bloomers? You'll likely want a selection of perennials and annuals.

How tall do they grow?

Do they need shade or sun?

What are their companions?

7. Arrange Your Plants

Now that you've made your decisions and done some research, it's time to arrange your plants.

AN ARRANGEMENT CHECKLIST

___ All plants are placed in the right amount of light, moisture, and soil.

___ Companion plants are close together.

___ Protector plants surround the garden. (More on this on page 22.)

___ Tall plants will not shade plants that need sun.

___ Tall plants won't block your view of the garden (if you don't want them to).

___ You've considered placing complementary colors near each other. (More on that in the "Color Magic" section starting on page 155.)

8. Seed Saving

Letting the last round of blooms go all the way through the flower's cycle will leave you with seeds. Once the blooms are wholly withered and dry, shaking the seeds into a bowl should be easy. A good tip is to bring a mixing bowl to the garden with you. Holding the bowl under it, break the flower (now a seedpod) from the stem. Let the whole pod fall into the bowl. Repeat this until you have collected the seeds from all the pods of a single species.

Later, you can sit and separate the seeds from the pods, sorting them into labeled containers. It's astonishing how many seeds a new flower produces—a humbling reminder that a single acorn can result in an entire forest.

Save the seeds somewhere dark and dry. Before it's time to plant them, find out if they will benefit from spending a week in the refrigerator first (like milkweed seeds) or the freezer (like mugwort).

This is called *proofing*. Proofing simulates the change in temperature from winter to spring, waking the seed so it's excited to grow.

Instead of proofing, you could store some of your seeds outside, sealed in a dark place. Let nature proof them for you, and see which seeds grow more happily.

Protecting the Garden with Magic

Traditional garden protections include:

1. Completing planting by adding three red flowers to the garden.

2. Create a ceremony of protection in which you place a lit candle in a jar in each of the four directions. Carrying a fifth candle, walk in a circle clockwise around the garden's perimeter, starting from the northmost point and singing a love song.

3. Tie red ribbons on trees that encircle the garden, whispering their names.

URBAN GARDENS

Follow a similar process to create a garden on a balcony, roof, or inside the kitchen window. Consider vertical designs for your garden. Where can they climb? What can stack?

Magical medicinal plants that thrive in containers can often be grown without seeds. Cuttings from produce that we buy at the deli can also provide us with plants, as long as they are properly encouraged and placed in the sun.

Save your glass jars! Most plants love to regenerate in a jar of water in indirect light or on a windowsill.

PLANT	TO GROW WITHOUT SEEDS	PROPERTIES
Aloe	Break off a leaf of the plant and place it in moist soil. It will root.	Heals burns
Basil	Place a cutting with two leaves in a jar of water. Plant in moist soil once roots emerge.	Protects from evil
Borage	Place a sprig within a jar of water. Plant in moist soil once roots emerge.	Merriment
Calendula	Place a cutting in a jar of water. Plant in moist soil once roots emerge.	Heals skin
Carrot	Place carrot tops on a plate of water. Do not submerge. Once they root, plant them and they will become tasty greens.	Fertility
Cayenne	Place a cutting with four leaves in moist soil. Roots will grow.	Insecticide
Celery	Chop off the bottom of the celery and rest it on top of a glass of water, submerging only the very bottom where the plant was cut. It will grow new roots below and celery stalks above.	Concentration, mental power
Chamomile	Place a sprig in a jar of water. Plant in moist soil once roots emerge.	Calming
Dandelion	Place a segment of dandelion root in warm, moist soil.	Healing
Echinacea	Place a sprig in a jar of water. Plant in moist soil once roots emerge.	Helps recovery from colds
Flowering bulbs	Plant in warm, moist soil.	Abundance

continued from previous page

PLANT	TO GROW WITHOUT SEEDS	PROPERTIES
Garlic	Rest the bulb on top of a glass of water, submerging only the very bottom. Once roots have sprouted, plant the bulb in moist soil.	Protection, supports immune system
Lavender	Place a sprig in a jar of water. Plant in moist soil once roots emerge.	Calm
Lemon balm	Place a sprig in a jar of water. Plant in moist soil once roots emerge.	Positivity
Mint	Place a sprig in a jar of water. Plant in moist soil once roots emerge.	Coolness, soothes stomach
Onion	Rest the bulb on top of a glass of water, submerging only the very bottom. Once roots have sprouted, plant the bulb in moist soil.	Absorbs negative energy
Potatoes	Once potato eyes show white nubs, cut the potato into pieces and place the pieces in warm, moist soil. Each nub will become a new plant.	Stability
Rosemary	Place a sprig in a jar of water. Plant in moist soil once roots emerge.	Memory
Sage	Place a sprig in a jar of water. Plant in moist soil once roots emerge.	Cleansing
Spinach	Place a sprig in a jar of water. Plant in moist soil once roots emerge.	Strength
Thyme	Place a sprig in a jar of water. Plant in moist soil once roots emerge.	Luck and protection
Turmeric	Place tuber in warm moist soil to regrow.	Reduces inflammation
Yarrow	Place a sprig in a jar of water. Plant in moist soil once roots emerge.	Psychic magic

Spell for Beauty

In winter,
the garden rattles brown bones,
dry stems
curved husks
enclosing
explosions
of seeds.

Breathing winter's garden
I sense
Winter's
rough rhythms
soft spectrums
bone shades
singing softly.

Repeat the last three lines as a mantra for seven days,
and notice the spell's effects when you look in the mirror:

I see
Nature's beauty
in me.

Part Two
HARVEST

Harvesting is a time of joy and abundance. Our fruits, vegetables, and flowers are evidence that we have completed a cycle of transformation. This application of energy to our intentions through collaboration with nature is the manifestation at the heart of Green Magic. Your book of magic (grimoire) will become a record of your growing knowledge of plants and their powers.

Hailing from varied climates, the plants chosen for this section offer magical, artistic, healing, and culinary applications. When they are nurtured by your hands, perhaps new, undiscovered dimensions of their power and beauty will be brought forth. Your grimoire will tell that story.

FLOWER GRIMOIRE

Note: This section contains references to color extraction processes described in more detail in Harnessing the Elements to Extract Plant Color, including smashing with a hammer or hapa zome (page 123), frozen baths (page 131), and steam eco-printing (page 125).

What Is a Grimoire?

Grimoire is a term used to describe a spell book. A spell is a process through which energy is applied to a situation to shift it. Some spells are incantations; some involve objects, drawings, or cooking. Spells take many forms, and different kinds of spells work best for different people.

For example, I work best with tarot cards and plants. Tarot cards help me focus my empathic powers to scry humans and their patterns. But others prefer a crystal ball or reading a flame. For spells, I best understand the ways that plants can shift energy and impact reality though their scents, flavors, chemistry, and ineffable magical qualities. I started to learn both of these skills from a young age, so I feel at home with them. However, you may encounter new forms of magic that you have never even heard of before that speak to you immediately and simply. Use whatever resonates with you, knowing that your magic may shift over time.

This book will cover all kinds of plant spells—and spells can be anything from inks (page 153) to herb bundles (page 168) to tinctures (page 180). As you experiment with plants, you can create your own grimoire, keeping track of the spells that work for you and the new combinations you invent. How do you feel when you work with specific plants? Does your experience of them shift depending on the time of year or weather? A grimoire can be a personal journal, an experimental log, and a recipe book. Later, you can review the pages to remember new spells, magical days, and milestones.

The Magic of Flowers

We were often running late when my oldest child started kindergarten, and I felt like a failure. Each morning, as I hurried her down the sidewalk, she would stop and insist on picking a purple flower from a bush, giving me a single bloom. One morning, I interrupted this ritual with a shrill "We are late!" She just blinked at me and picked the flower, pressing it into my palm. The plant was called "Yesterday, Today, Tomorrow," because, over time, the species' deep purple blooms fade to lavender, then to white, and then they are gone.

Floriography is the term for the language of flowers—their meanings defined according to the shared traditional understanding. But I think flowers speak in unison on one subject: enjoy the small, beautiful pleasures of life whenever you can.

I apologized to my wise kiddo. It never mattered that we were late for kindergarten. The flower ritual was far more important.

Flowers embody creation. They elevate us with their scents, softness, tastes, and colors. Across time and cultures, flowers and their hues have carried meanings central to the cycles and experiences of life. The flowers featured here have been cultivated for thousands of years by people worldwide to produce beautiful colors. They are magical, healing, and nutritious.

In the following pages, you will find instructions for accessing multiple paths to flower magic, including spells, gardening, healing, cooking, and

creating color baths. The spells here are drawn from texts from all over the world, dating back as far as the second century. You will see references to healing poultices, tinctures, flower essences, essential oils, and infused oils and waters.

Flower Essences

Employing flower essences for their healing and emotional properties stems from the ancient practice of gathering the dew that forms on blooms in the morning. One way to gather essences is to lay a cotton cloth over flowers in the morning, letting it soak up the dew. The fabric is then wrung out into a glass container and sealed.

Carrying, Wearing, and Sleeping with Flowers

Enhance the magic of flowers by putting them in your pocket, wearing them in your hair, or sleeping with them under your pillow. You can also carry flowers in pouches such as charm bags, sachets, or gris-gris, which can also go under your pillow. To create a simple pouch, lay your plants in the middle of a fabric square. Muslin, felt, or canvas are recommended, but any fabric you sense suits the spell will do. Consider the color, its meaning, and its relationship to your goals. (See page 163 for a chart of color meanings.) Gather the fabric square's corners and wrap it with an appropriately colored string or embroidery floss, tying it closed.

Flower Catalog

Arnica

Scientific Name: *Arnica*

Other Names: *Tlalyetl* (Nahuatl)

Colors: Yellow and green

Color Extraction: The hapa zome technique on cotton or silks is best.

Plant: Sun. Separate a piece of the arnica rhizome and place it in dry, poor soil. Arnica never likes to have wet roots.

Meaning: Power and resilience. Arnica is called wolf's bane or leopard's bane because it was thought to protect from these animals in the medieval world.

Healing Properties: *Arnica montana*'s essential oil, suspended in a 50 percent gel, is excellent for relieving muscle pain and healing bruises and swelling. You can find this at most stores that sell medicine. Do not ingest arnica. In large amounts, it is toxic.

Magic: Protection in the spirit and natural realms. Sprinkle arnica to safeguard the garden from harmful spirits. A circle of arnica plants can trap a spirit. Toss blossoms in the air to protect your home during storms. Create spiritual boundaries with lines of arnica. Make offerings of the blossoms to the fairies.

Other Traditional Uses: An ornamental plant in landscaping

Bee Balm

Scientific Name: *Monarda* (from the mint family Lamiaceae)

Other Names: Oswego tea, monarda, bergamot, horsemint

Colors: Pinks, peaches, and lavender

Color Extraction: Cover with water. Boil petals for one hour and then soak for twenty-four hours. Strain. Smashing, steeping, and freezing also work well.

Plant: Full sun to partial shade. Propagate by division every three years.

Meanings: Sympathy, clarity of thought, prosperity, and protection

Healing Properties: Antibacterial, antifungal, and anesthetic. Used in poultices and toothpaste.

Magic: Can be worn for protection against evil and illness. Burn bee balm in a fire to develop psychic powers, fertility, and good health.

Other Traditional Uses: Beloved in pollination gardens, bee balm can also help induce sweating at sweat lodges.

Black-Eyed Susan

Scientific Name: *Rudbeckia hirta*

Colors: Green golds and olive greens

Color Extraction: Keep flowers, seeds, and leaves separate. Cover with water. Simmer for thirty minutes and soak overnight before straining. Smashing and steeping work well. Copper and iron will deepen colors.

Plant: Full sun. Blooms in summer.

Meanings: Justice—perhaps because it blooms everywhere.

Healing Properties: The roots can be used as an immune booster like its cousin echinacea. Brewed into a tea, it guards against flu and colds by supporting the immune response.

Magic: Black-eyed Susans help the soul integrate light with shadow. They give us access to hidden aspects of our consciousness. Holding the seeds, say: "Show me what I cannot see."

Other Traditional Uses: Beloved in pollination gardens and as a cut flower. The Ojibwa people applied it as a poultice for snakebites.

Blue Butterfly Pea Flower

Scientific Name: *Clitoria ternatea*

Colors: Blues, greens, and purples

Color Extraction: Cover petals with water and boil for one hour. Soak for twenty-four hours. Strain. Smashing, steeping, and freezing followed by thawing also work well. Lemon juice may shift the color toward purple.

Plant: Full sun

Meanings: Let me go.

Healing Properties: Considered in Āyurveda to be memory-enhancing, antistress, antidepressant, anticonvulsant, and sedative. In traditional Chinese medicine, it is used to support the female libido. It brews into a beautiful blue tea.

Magic: Brewed in a tea, it supports transformation, serenity, love, and protection. Wearing fresh blooms attracts friendships. When carried in your hand, all will tell you the truth, and you will have courage and strength.

Other Traditional Uses: Revered as a holy flower, this plant is used to improve soil quality and as a food coloring.

Bougainvillea

Scientific Name: *Bougainvillea*

Colors: Bright pinks and fuchsia

Color Extraction: Cover petals with water and boil for one hour. Soak for twenty-four hours. Strain. Smashing, steeping, and freezing followed by thawing also work well.

Plant: Full sun. Bougainvillea loves salty air and propagates with tip cuttings.

Meanings: Passionate attraction

Healing Properties: Antioxidant

Magic: Give a stem to a loved one to ignite passion in your relationship.

Other Traditional Uses: The flower is edible and can be eaten in salads, deep fried, or brewed into drinks.

Calendula

Scientific Name: *Calendula officinalis*

Colors: Lemon yellow to olive greens

Color Extraction: Cover petals with water and bring to a low, gentle simmer for thirty minutes. Remove from heat and soak overnight. Strain. Smashing, steeping, and freezing followed by thawing also work well. Additives and mordants shift colors to green.

Plant: Full sun. It is said to bloom on the first days of the month.

Meanings: The joy and grief of remembrance

Healing Properties: Antioxidant. Do not combine with any sedative drugs.

Magic: Burning calendula over charcoal will support manifestation and love spells. Worn or used in tea, tincture, or oil, calendula will bring protection, abundance, and clear negativity.

Other Traditional Uses: Employed like saffron to color and flavor foods

Comfrey

Scientific Name: *Symphytum grandiflorum*

Other Names: Knitbone, boneset

Colors: Ochers to dark greens

Color Extraction: Cover petals with water and bring to a low, gentle simmer for thirty minutes. Strain. Smashing, steeping, and freezing followed by thawing also work well. Additives and mordants shift colors to green.

Plant: Full sun. Some do not go to seed and must be planted from cuttings in early fall or spring. Difficult to remove once planted.

Meanings: Grow together

Healing Properties: Not edible—do not ingest.

Magic: When worn, blooms provide safety during travels. The roots can be used in money spells. When burned with mugwort, comfrey can be used for divination.

Other Traditional Uses: Historically applied for the healing of broken bones

Coneflower

Scientific Name: *Echinacea purpurea*

Colors: Gold, olive green, and gray green

Color Extraction: Keep flowers, stems, and leaves separate. Cover petals with water and bring to a low, gentle simmer for thirty minutes. Steep for several days for the best results.

Plant: Full sun. Will tolerate partial shade.

Meanings: Justice

Healing Properties: Boosts the immune system when fighting colds, flu, and infection. Take it as tea or supplements.

Magic: When worn, it brings love. Placed under our pillow during sleep, the coneflower will return a lost love to you. Whoever picks the first flower of the season will experience uncontrollable lust.

Other Traditional Uses: Planted for prairie restoration

Coreopsis

Scientific Name: *Coreopsis*

Other Name: Tickseed

Colors: Yellows, oranges, browns, and reds

Color Extraction: Together, leaves, stems, and flowers will yield yellows, oranges, and browns. The petals alone, with an alkaline modifier, can produce red. Cover with water and simmer for thirty minutes. Soak overnight. Strain.

Plant: Full sun. Some are perennial. Deadhead—remove old dried blooms—to encourage new flowers. Deer resistant and drought tolerant.

Meanings: Persistent cheerfulness and love at first sight

Healing Properties: The roots are used for tea for diarrhea and as an emetic.

Magic: When worn, the blooms bring good luck and protect against lightning strikes.

Other Traditional Uses: Early leaves can be added to salads. The Navajo make a sacred lotion from the plant for treating many ailments, such as sprains and swelling.

Cosmos

Scientific Name: *Cosmos* from the Asteraceae family

Other Name: Mexican aster

Colors: Copper, orange, golden yellow, and gray green

Color Extraction: Cover flowers with water and simmer for one hour. Strain. Add soda ash to shift to yellow. Add iron for gray green.

Plant: Full sun, except for in extreme heat. Deadhead to encourage blooms.

Meanings: Order and harmony

Healing Properties: Cosmos have antihypertensive, anti-inflammatory, bone-protective, and antimicrobial properties. Only the *Cosmos sulphureus* are edible.

Magic: Plant in the garden to attract fairies. A gift of cosmos will bring good luck. Meditating with cosmos will enable you to hear messages from beyond.

Other Traditional Uses: An excellent cut flower with a long bloom season, *Cosmos sulphureus* can brighten salads.

Dahlia

Scientific Name: *Dahlia*

Colors: Yellows, oranges, and greens

Color Extraction: Cover flowers with water and simmer for forty minutes. Leave to steep overnight. Heat again for twenty minutes and leave to cool before straining. There should be enough pigment in the water that it is opaque. If it's still transparent, add more flowers and bring it to a simmer again. Smashing, steeping, and freezing followed by thawing also work well.

Plant: Full sun. Perennial except in cold climates.

Meanings: Steadfastness

Healing Properties: Dahlia tubers are a good source of insulin.

Magic: Used in spells for self-esteem and respect. Dahlias help us to see ourselves as others do. Carried, they protect against deceit, granting the power to see through the masks others wear.

Other Traditional Uses: The petals and bulbs are a staple of Oaxacan cuisine. The Aztecs used it to treat convulsions.

Dandelion

Scientific Name: *Taraxacum* from the Asteraceae family

Colors: Yellows and greens (flowers); pinks and purples (roots)

Color Extraction: It's best to use fresh flowers. Cover with water and simmer for thirty minutes.

Plant: Thrives everywhere.

Meanings: Order and harmony

Healing Properties: Supports blood sugar management and boosts skin, liver, and heart health. Treats constipation and improves digestive health.

Magic: Dandelion root tea aids in divination. Kept beside the bed, the tea will result in prophetic dreaming and call spirits. Buried near the northwest corner of the house, dandelions bring favorable winds. To send a message to a loved one, blow the seed head in their direction while visualizing your message.

Other Traditional Uses: Leaves, roots, and flowers are edible and excellent sources of vitamins and minerals. Dandelion root can be brewed into tea or eaten whole. Dandelion wine is made from fermented blooms.

Daylily

Scientific Name: *Hemerocallis*

Colors: Greens

Color Extraction: Cover blooms with boiling water and steep them for twenty-four hours.

Plant: Full sun or partial shade

Meanings: Desire, success, and forgetting painful past events

Healing Properties: Used as a tea to cure insomnia, reduce anxiety and stress, and treat coughs and fevers. The essential oils are said to alleviate depression.

Magic: Casting spells with lilies is easy. Simply give them as a gift. Gifted lilies help recipients forget worries, overcome troubling times, and move on. The smell promotes happiness and tranquility.

Other Traditional Uses: The flower is edible. It contains vitamin C and protein.

Dyer's Chamomile

Scientific Name: *Anthemis tinctoria*

Other Name: Golden marguerite

Colors: Greens, yellow, buff, and golden orange

Color Extraction: Pick the flowers once they begin to wilt. Simmer for thirty minutes and soak overnight. The flowers give lightfast warm yellows and oranges. Harvest the leaves and stalks year-round to produce different shades of greens.

Plant: Full sun to partial shade

Meanings: Energy in adversity

Healing Properties: Unlike chamomile, golden marguerite doesn't possess significant medicinal properties.

Magic: A hand wash with dyer's chamomile will help gamblers ensure winnings. When sprinkled around your property, the blooms undo curses and spells cast against you. Add to your bath to attract love.

Other Traditional Uses: When chamomiles are planted next to a weak plant, both will begin to thrive.

Fuchsia

Scientific Name: *Fuchsia*

Colors: Hot pinks and purples

Color Extraction: Simmer flowers for about an hour until the pigment fades from the petals. Stir and strain.

Plant: Full sun to partial shade

Meanings: Discernment, playfulness, and uplift

Healing Properties: The flower essences are said to support the release of sadness.

Magic: Meditate with fuchsia to access long-repressed emotions and release long-held grief.

Other Traditional Uses: The entire fuchsia plant is edible.

Goldenrod

Scientific Name: *Solidago odora*

Colors: Bright yellows to deep greens

Color Extraction: Simmer for forty-five minutes and leave overnight to cool. Strain. For yellow, add an alum. For a sage/olive green, add an iron solution.

Plant: Full sun to partial shade

Meanings: Precaution

Healing Properties: Goldenrod may be anti-inflammatory, antiseptic, and lower blood pressure. It may help with urinary tract health.

Magic: To see your future love, wear a piece of goldenrod. When held in hand, the bloom nods toward hidden or lost objects—including hidden treasure. If goldenrod springs up by the door, it means unexpected good fortune for the family.

Other Traditional Uses: The flowers are edible. Make tea with them and the leaves. The leaves can also be cooked and added to recipes that call for spinach.

Hibiscus

Scientific Name: *Hibiscus sabdariffa*

Other Names: Kharkady, rosella and Jamaican sorrel, Florida cranberry

Colors: Light pink, magenta to purple, dark blue, black, and occasionally green

Color Extraction: Cover the flowers with water, simmer for thirty minutes, and then strain.

Plant: Full sun to partial shade

Meanings: Precaution

Healing Properties: High in vitamin C and antioxidants, hibiscus boosts the immune system.

Magic: Hibiscus tea induces lust. Added to sachets or incense, it works as a love spell. Float flowers in a bowl during divination spells.

Other Traditional Uses: The flower, fruit, and leaves are all edible.

Hollyhock (Black)

Scientific name: *Alcea*

Colors: Mint green, gray purple, mustard

Color Extraction: Cover blossoms with water and simmer until the water turns dark purple and the petals have faded. Darker flower heads yield saturated colors. Use fresh or dried.

Plant: Full sun to partial shade. Moist soil and compost.

Meaning: The circle of life

Healing Properties: Hollyhocks alleviate pain, treat stomach ulcers, heal wounds, and treat diabetes.

Magic: To make a poppet, strip the green sepals off a hollyhock bud and then stick the stem of an open flower into the folds of the bud's petals. Hollyhocks extend to the realm of fairies. To see fairies, combine hollyhocks, marigolds, wild thyme, and hazel buds.

Other Traditional Uses: The flower, fruit, and leaves are all edible. A stalk of hollyhocks can be incorporated into celebrations of Lammas to ensure the fertility of fields.

Hopi Sunflower

Scientific Name: *Helianthus annuus macrocarpus*

Other Name: *Tceqa' Qu' Si* (Hopi)

Colors: Silvery-gray, gray, purple, blue, black, and bright yellow

Color Extraction: Cover the seeds or petals with water. Bring to a boil and gently simmer for half an hour or until the seeds split open. Strain. The seeds create purple, blue, and black, shifting with additives. Petals yield bright yellow.

Plant: Full sun, rich soil, and moderate soil moisture

Meaning: Wishes and beautiful surroundings

Healing Properties: Used in snakebite poultices

Magic: If you cut a sunflower at sunset while making a simple wish, it will come true before another nightfall. Sleeping with a sunflower under the bed reveals the truth about something you find mysterious. Sunflower seed patterns form the Fermat spiral, following the golden ratio. This is the spiral in our DNA and in the Milky Way. Most sunflowers have exactly 55 or 144 seeds.

Other Traditional Uses: Planted on the north edges of gardens as a "fourth sister" to the Three Sisters companion plants of corn, beans, and squash. Eat the seeds raw or roasted. Not for those who are allergic to sunflower oil. Sunflowers remove toxic substances and radiation from the soil.

Lavender

Scientific Name: *Lavandula*

Colors: Cool green and lavender

Color Extraction: Hapa zome techniques work best.

Plant: Sun

Meaning: Elegance, serenity, grace

Healing Properties: Used to calm emotions and skin. Antiseptic. Used with feverfew to create a tincture to treat headaches.

Magic: Can be added to any spell to calm, reduce stress, bring balance, and open intuition. Used as oils, teas, baths, smudges, talismans, and more. An amulet of lavender will help you speak to ghosts.

Other Traditional Uses: To bake with lavender, use *Lavandula angustifolia*—the English variety. An easy way to incorporate lavender into cooking without its flavor becoming overwhelming is to mix dried flowers into sugar, letting the oils infuse it. Then use this lavender sugar in cookies and cakes.

Lupine

Scientific Name: *Lupinus*

Colors: Yellows (stalk) and greens (flowers and roots)

Color Extraction: Cover with water and boil for thirty minutes. Let sit overnight. Strain. The stalk and the leaves produce yellow hues. Adding in the flowers and roots yield a temporary green.

Plant: Full sun or partial shade in sandy, well-drained soil and cool temperatures

Meaning: Named for how much wolves love them. They represent imagination, admiration, and overall happiness.

Magic: Planting lupines brings luck to the gardener. They prevent misfortune and disease in the home. Press lupine blooms and keep them close to your heart when frightened.

Other Traditional Uses: Only the seeds are edible. They can be ground into flour. Lupines are nitrogen-fixing and can improve your soil.

Marigold

Scientific Name: *Tagetes*

Other Names: *Cempasúchil, cemooalxochiyl* (Nahuatl), *maravilla* (Spanish)

Colors: Oranges, yellows, greens, and maroon

Color Extraction: To extract color, smashing, freezing, and simmering for thirty minutes all work well. Frozen marigolds can be stewed in warm water in a jar set in the sun. Separate the flower petals to obtain a clear golden yellow. Use the entire plant at the season's end (minus the roots) to get greener shades.

Plant: Full sun planted in spring. Harvest in fall.

Meaning: Grief or, with cypress, despair

Healing Properties: When applied topically, the calendula variety of marigolds supports healthy skin. Tinctures can be made by suspending the blossoms in olive oil.

Magic: Picked at noon, marigolds will strengthen and comfort the heart. Garlands hung on the door will stop evil from entering. Scattered under the bed, they protect you while you sleep and give you prophetic dreams. According to legend, if a girl's bare feet touch marigold petals, she will understand all the bird languages.

Other Traditional Uses: Marigold petals are edible and can be added to salads. During Dia de los Muertos celebrations, marigolds are placed on the *ofrenda* and are referred to as the *flor de muerto* or flowers of the dead. Their scent will attract souls to the family altar. Marigolds protect nearby plants from insects and nematodes, making them good companion plants for tomatoes, eggplant, and chili peppers.

Marjoram

Scientific Name: *Origanum majorana* or *O. vulgare*

Other Name: Joy of the mountain

Colors: Yellows and greens

Color Extraction: Cover with water. Simmer for thirty minutes and leave to soak overnight. Strain.

Plant: Full sun

Meaning: You make me blush.

Healing Properties: Marjoram has anti-inflammatory, antimicrobial, and antioxidant properties. The scent promotes hormonal balance and anxiety relief.

55

Magic: Used in love spells and added to food to strengthen love. It is protective when carried or placed around the house—a bit in each room renewed monthly. In the garden, it shields against evil. Wear with violet in winter as an amulet against colds.

Other Traditional Uses: Use marjoram as a substitute for oregano in cooking. Brew fresh or dried marjoram leaves into tea.

Mexican Tarragon/Pericón

Scientific Name: *Tagetes lucida*

Other Name: *Yiauhtli* (Nahuatl)

Colors: Yellows, golds

Color Extraction: Simmer flowers for thirty minutes and soak overnight. Strain. Or use the sun bath method.

Plant: Sun

Meaning: Weed of the clouds. Important to Tlaloc, the Aztec god of the rain and giver of life. Traces of ancient offerings of *yiauhtli* remain in the Tlaloc's Templo Mayor.

Healing Properties: Antibiotic and settling the stomach

Magic: Brings rain and vitality. Use the blossoms in altars to bring rain. Carry the blossoms or dyed cloths with you to keep your energy up.

Other Traditional Uses: Burn dried flowers and leaves as an insect repellent. They make incense and offerings in the festivities dedicated to the god of rain. Pericón flowers are used to make crosses to mark the festival for the battle between San Miguel and the Devil.

Morning Glory and Wild Sweet Potato

Scientific Names: *Ipomoea purpurea* and *Ipomoea pandurata*, respectively

Other Name: Binding weed

Colors: Blue, pink, purple, and green

Color Extraction: To extract color, smashing, freezing, and simmering for one hour all work well. Morning glory and wild sweet potato can be stewed in warm water in a jar set in the sun. Adding alum stabilizes the bath and shifts the color to green—the traditional way to make textile dye from wild sweet potato.

Plant: Full sun. They are perennials but behave as annuals in cold climates.

Meaning: Affection

Healing Properties: A poultice from the wild sweet potato root can ease joint pain, while a tea brewed from the roots may have laxative effects.

Magic: Grown in the garden, morning glory brings peace, strength, and happiness. Place its seeds under your pillow to halt nightmares. When starting a new project, use your morning glory pigment to write about your hopes during the new moon on a slip of paper. Wrap the paper with the blooms.

Other Traditional Uses: The wild sweet potato has roots that resemble sweet potatoes. The roots can be steamed and eaten. The morning glory is not edible, and its seeds may have a psychotropic effect if ingested. They are considered toxic.

Mugwort

Scientific Name: *Artemisia vulgaris*

Colors: Warm yellow and brown

Color Extraction: The hapa zome technique has beautiful results on cotton. Also, leaves and flowers can be simmered for thirty minutes and steeped overnight.

Plant: Sun

Meaning: Happiness and the moon

Healing Properties: Thought to aid digestion, menstruation, and liver function. Can be made into a poultice to boost energy, calm nerves, support digestion, and relieve itching and pain.

Magic: Thought to offer protection of the spirit, mind, heart, and body. Hung over the doorway or worn as a talisman, it will keep evil spirits and illness away. Sewn into a pillow with agrimony, mugwort is said to help overcome fear and negative emotions and reverse spells. Burned or drunk as a tea to increase psychic abilities.

Other Traditional Uses: Ingested to promote relaxation and vivid dreams, mugwort can also flavor savory dishes.

Passion Flower

Scientific Name: *Passiflora incarnata*

Colors: Violet, bright yellow, and deep green

Color Extraction: Simmer for thirty minutes and soak overnight. Fruit skins create violet. Alum shifts to green.

Plant: Full sun

Meaning: Religious superstition

Healing Properties: A dietary supplement for anxiety and sleep problems. Applied to the skin for burns.

Magic: Placed in the home to calm problems and bring peace. Carried, it attracts friends and enhances popularity. Kept under the pillow, passion flower aids sleep.

Other Traditional Uses: Both fruits and flowers are edible and sweet.

Poppy

Scientific Name: *Papaver*

Colors: California: soft yellow, green, teal, gray; red poppy: blue, fuchsia, purple, dark blue to gray

Color Extraction: Separate leaves and petals. Cover with water. Simmer until petals fade (about an hour). Strain. Or soak in the sunlight. Smashing and freezing followed by thawing also work well.

Plant: Full sun

Meaning: Red poppies mean consolation. Scarlet poppies mean fantastic extravagance. White poppies mean "I need sleep, but my dreams are troubled."

Healing Properties: Aids in sleep and with sore throats

Magic: Carried, poppies promote fertility and attract good fortune. To disappear, place these items between two candles: poppy seeds for invisibility, cloves for protection and to cause confusion, and glass for transparency.

Other Traditional Uses: Poppies are edible. The flowers and seeds can be used fresh in salads or baked goods.

Purple Basil

Scientific Name: *Ocimum basilicum L.*

Other name: Witch weed

Colors: Golden yellow and green

Color Extraction: Cover flowers with water and simmer for thirty minutes. Soak overnight for a golden yellow. For green, add the leaves and stalks.

Plant: Full sun

Meaning: Hatred

Healing Properties: Purple basil is an excellent source of potassium that supports blood clotting and bone strength. Basil oils boost the immune system and healthy skin.

Magic: Spread leaves over the floors to banish evil from your home. Eat basil on Tuesday for strength in battle. Eat basil on Wednesday to start a dialogue.

Other Traditional Uses: Edible, it can be eaten like green basils. Witches were said to drink a half cup of basil juice before taking flight.

Purple Pincushion Flower

Scientific Name: *Scabiosa*

Colors: Lavender, purple, green, and dark blue. With additives, grayish, teal greens, and bright pinks.

Color Extraction: Cover with water. Boil for thirty to sixty minutes, and soak overnight. Strain. Experiment with additives.

Plant: Full sun

Meaning: Unfortunate love

Healing Properties: Used topically for eye problems, heartburn, respiratory problems, wounds, and skin infections

Magic: For psychic powers, lightly crush the flowers and rub them on your forehead. When grown by the door of the house, the plant brings good luck and keeps fevers at bay.

Other Traditional Uses: Edible and good in salads

Rose

Scientific Name: *Rosa*

Colors: Pink, fuchsia, purple, blue, or black (petals); gray and black (rose hips); yellow-green to deep green (leaves and stems)

Color Extraction: Cover with water and simmer for thirty minutes to one hour. Soak overnight.

Plant: Full sun

Meanings:
  Red: Love and perfection
  White: Innocence and purity
  Burgundy: Grace, elegance, joyfulness
  Yellow: Friendship, warmth, happiness
  Orange: Desire, passion, romantic fervor
  Lavender: Enchantment and love at first sight

Healing Properties: Rose hips and petals can be made into a tincture that relieves headaches.

Magic: Roses grow best when stolen. Roses planted in the garden attract fairies. To cast a love spell: on a full moon, walk around your dwelling thrice, sprinkling rose petals and repeating, "Come to me. I'm prepared for you." Rose petals scattered inside the house calm stress and household upheavals. Wear rose hips as love-attracting beads. Rose oil will bring quick luck. A rosebud tea drunk before sleep will induce prophetic dreams.

Other Traditional Uses: The leaf, bud, petal, and hip of rose plants are edible. Use rose petals in desserts, jellies, syrups, butter, and teas. Rose hips are used in jams, wines, teas, sauces, and soups. Rose leaves can be brewed into a tea similar to black tea.

Safflower

Scientific Name: *Carthamus tinctorius*

Colors: Bright yellow and pinks

Color Extraction: For yellow, cover the flowers with water, simmer for thirty minutes to an hour, and strain. For pink, return the liquid to the pot and add washing soda. Strain and add vinegar or lemon juice until the liquid turns bright red.

Plant: Full sun

Meaning: Good luck and happiness

Healing Properties: The acids in safflower seed oil support heart health, lower cholesterol, and reduce the risk of heart disease.

Magic: To attract male lovers, burn the flowers with charcoal as incense, sprinkle petals around your bedroom, or carry the flowers with you.

Other Traditional Uses: Use in cooking as a saffron substitute. Add to a bath to moisturize your skin.

Saint-John's-Wort

Scientific Name: *Hypericum perforatum*

Other Names: Klamath weed, goatweed

Colors: Greens and maroons

Color Extraction: Cover the flowers with water and simmer for thirty minutes, or soak them in warm water in the sun for a full day.

Plant: Full sun to partial shade

Meaning: Animosity and superstition

Healing Properties: Saint-John's-wort is taken as a supplement for depression. Applied to the skin, Saint-John's-wort has been used to treat wounds, bruises, and muscle pain.

Magic: Worn, the flowers ward off fevers and colds, make soldiers invincible, and attract love.

Other Traditional Uses: Can be brewed into teas.

Sour Grass

Scientific Name: *Oxalis pes-caprae*

Other Names: Bermuda buttercup, wood sorrel

Colors: Yellow and orange

Color Extraction: Cover the flowers and stems with water. Heat gently for thirty minutes or allow to steep. The water will turn from clear to bright yellow.

Plant: Partial to full sun

Meaning: Joy and good-heartedness

Healing Properties: Used as a diuretic, coolant, astringent, and stomach soother. Make the flowers into a poultice to reduce swelling.

Magic: Carry the leaves to protect your heart. Fresh flowers placed in the sickroom speed recovery from illness and injury.

Other Traditional Uses: Sour grass is high in vitamin C. Ingest in moderation because it is also high in oxalic acid, which can be toxic.

Sticky Monkey Flower

Scientific Name: *Mimulus aurantiacus*

Colors: Yellows and grays

Color Extraction: Cover branches, leaves, and flowers with water and simmer until their color fades. Strain.

Plant: Full to partial sun

Meaning: Presumption

Healing Properties: Said to cool the skin and soothe the stomach, it can be used as a diuretic or an astringent.

Magic: Meditating on this flower addresses issues of the second chakra: sexuality and relationships. Breathing in while focusing on the blossoms will build confidence, warmth, and connection.

Other Traditional Uses: The leaves, flowers, and seedpods are edible. The leaves can be brewed into tea or used in salads, soups, and sauces.

Sumac

Scientific Name: *Rhus*

Other Name: Summaq

Colors: Yellow, orange, and green (bark); purple, yellow, and tan (leaves)

Color Extraction: Cut the sumac berries. Boil for one to one and a half hours and then strain. Add to a steaming iron bath for thirty minutes to achieve a dark gray.

Plant: Best in full sun, will grow in partial shade.

Meaning: Nature's wildness

Healing Properties: Antiviral, antimicrobial, anti-inflammatory, and antioxidant

Magic: Create peace by adding sumac leaves and berries to a bottle of water. If you have already been found guilty in court, gather up nine sumac berries and put them in your pocket for a lighter sentence.

Other Traditional Uses: Sumac is used in dry rubs, spice blends like za'atar, and dressings.

Tansy

Scientific Name: *Tanacetum vulgare*

Other Name: Buttons

Colors: Bright yellows and a range of greens

Color Extraction: Chop the tansy flower tops into small pieces and cover them with water. Simmer in the dye pot for one to two hours.

Plant: Full sun to light shade. Frost tolerant.

Meaning: I declare war against you.

Healing Properties: Tansy is made into poultices for skin diseases. Poisonous if ingested.

Magic: Place leaves in your shoes to cure fevers. Carry it for longevity.

Other Traditional Uses: Tansies keep ants away.

Vervain

Scientific Name: *Verbena*

Other Names: Simpler's joy, holy herb, wild hyssop, *mǎ biān cǎo* (Chinese)

Colors: Blue, purple, and green

Color Extraction: Smashing, steeping, and freezing followed by thawing work well.

Plant: Sun

Meaning: Enchantment, the day

Healing Properties: Vervain is thought to have anti-inflammatory, antibacterial, antispasmodic, and analgesic effects. It may ease anxiety and insomnia.

Magic: Considered a powerful magical herb across the ancient world, it is used in teas, baths, and incense to bring joy, love, vision, and clarity.

Other Traditional Uses: The seeds can be roasted and ground into a flour.

Woad (Seeds)

Scientific Name: *Isatis tinctoria*

Other Name: Glastum

Colors: Gray, tan, cool light pink, and eggshell. Freshly picked, newly darkened seeds will produce a light blue color.

Color Extraction: Simmer the seeds for an hour or so. Cool before straining.

Plant: Full sun

Meaning: Protection, courage

Healing Properties: Used to stem bleeding and protect against infection

Magic: Protection, courage. Use the stem and root to create magic wands.

Other Traditional Uses: Ancient Egyptians used woad to dye cloth wrappings for mummies. Ancient Celtic warriors used it for staining or tattooing themselves blue.

Yarrow

Scientific Name: *Achillea millefolium*

Other Names: Arrowroot, bad man's plaything, death flower, devil's nettle, and eerie

Colors: Pale yellows, beiges, and light olive greens are possible with different mordants and modifiers.

Color Extraction: Used fresh or dried. Cover with water and simmer for ninety minutes.

Plant: Full sun

Meaning: Unconditional love

Healing Properties: Yarrow may improve digestion and treat cramps.

Magic: When worn, yarrow protects and attracts love, friends, distant relations, and those you miss. When held in your hand, yarrow transforms fear into courage. The flower ensures that love will last seven years when hung over the bed or altar. Yarrow tea improves psychic powers.

Other Traditional Uses: Edible peppery foliage and bitter leaves are added to salads.

Zinnia

Scientific Name: *Zinnia* from the family Asteraceae

Colors: Yellows and browns

Color Extraction: Cover with water and simmer for two and a half hours to extract the pigment from the flowers. Squeeze before straining.

Plant: Full sun. Cut blooms above new buds to keep them blooming. Annual.

Meaning: Thoughts of an absent friend

Magic: Use them in spells for strength, health, endurance, or abundance. On orange fabric, place a red candle to the right and a bouquet of zinnias on the left. Say, "I call upon all the power I have within. I face my struggles. I fight until I win." Blow out the candle. Keep the zinnias until they wilt.

Other Traditional Uses: Zinnias are grown as cut flowers, constantly replace their blooms, and are excellent in pollination gardens.

TREES, HERBS, AND ROOTS GRIMOIRE

There isn't a single herb or spice that doesn't have a constellation in the heavens that strikes it and tells it to grow.
—*MIDRASH,* BERESHIT RABBAH 10

Across cultures, people believe that the movement of the heavens affects events on earth. Like all of us, redwoods—beings so complex that their DNA sequence is nine times longer than ours—are made of stardust. Sometimes, entire redwoods forests move slowly, echoing the heavens, migrating over thousands of years, spreading to new, more favorable environments.

Or sometimes, like meteors, they move suddenly. A mudslide tears their shallow roots from a mountainside. After they fall, new trees will spring from the horizontal trunks. In time, the forest will have moved to a new valley, establishing roots and continuing its life.

Wherever the forest moves, it takes complex ecosystems with it. In the redwood forest's upper story, entangled communities of animals, plants, and lichens thrive, never touching the ground. Below, the redwoods nurture salmon, cleaning the water, shading and protecting their eggs, and eventually, after their massive trunks have fallen, damming the streams to create deep, safe pools for them to spawn. When the salmon die, their bodies' nutrients will nurture the redwoods' new growth.

About redwoods, John Steinbeck wrote:

From them comes silence and awe. It's not only their unbelievable stature, nor their color which seems to shift and vary under your eyes, no, they are not like any trees we know, they are ambassadors from another time.

Celtic Tree Astrology

Perhaps these dynamic interrelationships inspired Celtic tree astrology. The redwood's Irish cousin, hazel, is said to have first grown over the magical Well of Wisdom. With branches that stretched high into the sky and roots that plunged deep into the earth, the tree held all the knowledge of the universe. Among its roots, salmon thrived, protected and nurtured. Celtic stories say the tree passed its knowledge on to salmon through its hazelnuts. The salmon ate the nuts and learned from the tree. The people ate the salmon and learned, too.

The ancient Irish believed trees were home to the spirits of their ancestors and bridges to the Otherworld. They recognized each tree's unique spiritual properties.

Celtic culture has birth signs and seasons like Vedic, Hebrew, and Western astrology star signs. Theirs credits the nature of each life's path to the trees.

Celtic Tree Astrology Birth Signs

BIRTHDAYS	TREE	TRAITS	ANIMAL GUARDIAN	GEMSTONE
December 24–January 20	Birch	The Achiever: Motivated, ambitious, passionate	Golden eagle, white stag	Quartz crystal
January 21–February 17	Rowan	The Thinker: Progressive, creative, original, visionary, moral	Green dragon	Peridot
February 18–March 17	Ash	The Enchanter: Freethinker, creative, imaginative, intuitive, spontaneous	Seal, seahorse, seagull	Coral
March 18–April 14	Alder	The Trailblazer: Early adopter, innovator, discoverer	Bear, fox, hawk	Ruby

continued from previous page

BIRTHDAYS	TREE	TRAITS	ANIMAL GUARDIAN	GEMSTONE
April 15– May 12	Willow	The Observer: Creative, intuitive, intelligent, adaptive	Adder, hare, sea serpent	Moonstone
May 13– June 9	Hawthorn	The Illusionist: Wise, spiritual, perceptive, compassionate, calm	Bee, owl	Topaz
June 10– July 7	Oak	The Stabilizer: Fair, confident, positive	Wren, otter, white horse	Diamond
July 8– August 4	Holly	The Ruler: Noble, successful, brave	Cat, unicorn	Carnelian
August 5– September 1	Hazel	The Knower: Seeks and carries knowledge	Crane, salmon	Amethyst
September 2– September 29	Vine	The Equalizer: Adaptable, unpredictable, strong-spirited	Lizard, hound, white swan	Emerald
September 30– October 27	Ivy	The Resilient One: Charismatic, restless, optimistic, collaborative	Boar, butterfly, goose	Opal
October 28– November 24	Reed	The Leader: Strong, history lover, lifelong learner	Hound, owl	Jasper
November 25– December 23	Elder	The Scholar: Free-spirited, risky, self-interested, resilient	Badger, black horse, raven	Jet

Celtic Tree Calendar

Many pagan cultures mark the passage of time on a circular calendar called the Wheel of the Year. Shaping the calendar as a circle reflects nature's repeating and connected cycles. The Celtic tree astrology calendar is most often depicted as a wheel. The seasons of the trees have strong relationships to calendars in Vedic and Hebrew astrology.

Birch Season: December 24–January 20. If you are struggling, remember the light. The sun will always come again, and nature is reborn. Now is a time of nurturing your creativity, healing, and preparing.

Rowan Season: January 21–February 17. Moving from the quiet of the birch season, rowan is the time to step into your power, pursuing your goals with success. Stay connected to the wisdom you've gathered over the seasons.

Ash Season: February 18-March 17. Now that you have momentum, pause and focus on the inner self. This is the season of magical intuition. Pay attention to your nighttime dreams. What are they telling you?

Alder Season: March 18-April 14. Now that you have reflected, it is time to apply your intuitive understanding and make spiritual decisions. You are finding balance. What will nourish your spirit?

Willow Season: April 15-May 12. You are loving and nurturing, and your spirit is strong. Focus on healing, learning, and creating.

Hawthorn Season: May 13-June 9. A time of new beginnings. Find new love, grow your family, make business decisions, or develop a new dimension of your career.

Oak Season: June 10-July 7. A lucky time. Look for falling oak leaves. Catch one, and you'll be healthy all year. Carried in your pocket, acorns will bring you luck. Your energy expands. Your actions are rooted in your wisdom.

Holly Season: July 8-August 4. Your energy moves in cycles like nature. Holly can connect us to luck, protection, and nature's immortality. Clean your space to prepare for bounty and abundance.

Hazel Season: August 5-September 1. Now is a time of bounty and abundance. Commune with your muse, and you will be productive and experience creative flow.

Vine Season: September 2-September 29. This is the season of passionate emotions. Celebrate nature's magic, joy, and wonder. You are growing. Prepare to experience your shadow side and work toward balance.

Ivy Season: September 30-October 27. Recognize what sustains you, and banish the negative. Bind yourself to things that nourish you and let go of what doesn't serve. Your intuition is especially strong in this season.

Reed Season: October 28-November 24. This is an excellent time to connect with ancestors and those in the Otherworld. Develop your ability to scry. Clearing and cleansing spells are powerful in this season, helping you stay on your true path.

Elder Season: November 25-December 23. This is the time of endings that become new beginnings and setbacks that become opportunities. Your connection to nature adds to your resilience.

Trees, Herbs, and Roots Catalog

The Celts and Druids focused on the trees they knew and lived among to develop their calendar system. Those trees have relatives all over the world. All trees are complex beings who nourish each other and us; they are always here for you. What follows is an index of selected trees, herbs, and roots and a series of strategies for engaging magic through them.

SCRY A TREE

Each tree is a unique character. To get to know a tree, stand tall as you observe it.

1) Recognize the earth beneath your feet, grounding yourself. Visualize your spine as a string of pearls being tugged straight from the top of your head to the base of your tailbone. Breathe.

2) Next scry the stance of the tree. Which way does it lean? Adjust your body to lean this way. Now you understand the tree's relationship with the wind.

3) Look for the spiral of the tree's branches. Like galaxies and DNA, tree branches emerge in a spiral pattern. When you have found it, you have located the tree's heart. Place your palm over your heart.

4) Look at the neighboring trees. They are conversing and sharing nourishment through their roots in collaboration with the fungi surrounding them. These trees are not competing. They are working together. Now you know your tree's community.

5) If you find smaller trees of the same species surrounding your tree, your tree is a mother. She will put her children's needs before her own, sending them carbon under the ground. If your tree is not a mother, see if you can find the mother tree and wrap your arms around her.

Tree love will heal your heart.

Acorn

Scientific Name: *Quercus*

Colors: Silver from acorn caps, gray (with iron bath). Can be used as a mordant.

Color Extraction: Please see the Acorn Cap Ink recipe on page 137.

Plant: Full sun to partial shade

Myths and Meanings: Each acorn contains the possibility of a mighty oak forest. Gifts of acorns remind a loved one of their potential.

Healing Properties: Appropriately prepared, acorns support digestion, promote heart health, and have antibacterial and antiviral properties.

Magic: The seeds of oaks, acorns bring good luck. Carried or placed on a windowsill, acorns ward off evil and attract prosperity and health. Acorns gathered at night may increase fertility.

Other Traditional Uses: Raw acorns are unsafe to ingest. Boiling or soaking them can remove their toxic tannins. Properly prepared acorns are edible and can be roasted or ground into flour.

Aloe

Scientific Name: *Aloe vera*

Color: Pink. Can be used as a mordant.

Color Extraction: Sun baths work well. Break the leaves and drop them into a jar. Cover the leaves with water and set the jar in the sun.

Plant: Full sun to partial shade

Myths and Meanings: In ancient Egypt, aloe was considered the "plant of immortality."

Healing Properties: Has antioxidant and antibacterial properties. The gel in its leaves soothes burns and eases digestion.

Magic: Planted outside the home alone brings good luck and prosperity while banishing envy and negativity.

Other Traditional Uses: A powerful air-purifying plant. The insides of the leaves can be eaten raw, gently poached, or blanched for a milder taste. It contains vitamins A, C, and E. Also used in natural hair dyes.

Apple (Leaves and Bark)

Scientific Name: *Malus domestica*

Colors: Yellow and pinks

Color Extraction: Simmer leaves and bark for at least two hours and let them soak overnight.

Plant: Sun

Myths and Meanings: Long life that continues even through little deaths

Healing Properties: Apples are nutrient-dense, especially their skin, with vitamins C and E and antioxidants. High in fiber and water. Supports heart health. Place a thin slice of apple on a split lip.

Magic: Apples are associated with witches because they hide a pentacle at their core. They bring abundance, love, longevity, creativity, and fertility. An apple given or cooked with a specific intention is a magic spell.

Other Traditional Uses: For baking, cider-making, and vinegar

Apricot

Scientific Name: *Prunus armeniaca*

Colors: Yellow and green

Color Extraction: Simmer leaves for an hour.

Plant: Sun

Myths and Meanings: In Chinese culture, literary arts, courage and war, or beauty and innocence. In Japanese culture, love, passion, and perseverance. In Buddhist traditions, the flowers signify enlightenment, life's transience, and the temporary nature of existence. In Persian tradition, the flowers mean spring, new beginnings, renewal of life, and hope, and in the Victorian language of flowers, they mean admiration, gratitude, and friendship.

Healing Properties: Antioxidant and anti-inflammatory

Magic: Bake with apricots while imagining you are stirring love, romance, and passion. Serve.

Other Traditional Uses: Apricot flowers are given as gifts for the Korean celebration of the Lunar New Year to bring prosperity and success.

Birch

Scientific Name: *Betula*

Colors: Pink (bark), yellow (leaves)

Color Extraction: Heat to an almost-boil. Simmer one to two hours.

Plant: Full sun to partial shade

Myths and Meanings: Renewal

Healing Properties: Pain relief. Leaves and bark can treat sprains, sore muscles, and headaches. Steam leaves to clear sinuses. Birch tea treats stomach problems.

Magic: Psychic protection. Carried, it protects from malevolent fairies.

Other Traditional Uses: Birch is used for magical celebrations in pagan traditions, including Beltane fires, maypoles, and Yule logs. Birch is also used to make brooms for Yuletide. Celtic people made cribs from birch so it would protect their babies.

Blackthorn

Scientific Name: *Prunus spinosa*

Colors: Grays (bark) and yellows (shoots)

Color Extraction: Simmer for one hour, and then soak the bark for a week, using an iron mordant. Simmer blackthorn shoots for one hour and let soak overnight. Experiment with mordants to shift the yellows toward green.

Plant: Sun

Myths and Meanings: Linked with warfare, injury, and death. Associated with Cailleach (Scotland) and Morrigan, it symbolizes the Crone, keeper of dark secrets and the shadow side of magic. Blackthorn flowers usher in the Celtic celebration of Imbolc, which is dedicated to the goddess Brigid and the coming of spring. Fairies guard blackthorn and will burn down the house of anyone who cuts one down.

Healing Properties: Antioxidant, anti-inflammatory, antimicrobial. Supports cardiovascular system.

Magic: The wood is used to make powerful wands. Thorns are used in protection spells.

Other Traditional Uses: Blue-black fruits are called sloes and are used for making sloe gin. They can also be made into vinegar and jelly. In Britain, it is used to make a cattle-proof hedge. In Ireland, its wood is used to make shillelaghs.

Buckthorn

Scientific Name: *Rhamnus*

Colors: Yellow, green (ripened berries), pinkish-red (bark), blue (berry skins)

Color Extraction: Yellow: Boil leaves for at least thirty minutes. Green: Simmer whole ripe berries. (See ink recipe on page 138.) Pinks and reds: Simmer buckthorn bark. Blue: Squeeze berries and remove skins, placing them in a jar. Cover with water and leave in the sun.

Plant: Full sun to partial shade

Myths and Meanings: Beauty and vitality. The air. Sea buckthorn leaves were the preferred food of the mythical winged horse Pegasus, helping with flight.

Healing Properties: Use alder buckthorn to calm skin, including burns, eczema, acne, and wrinkles.

Magic: Buckthorn bark drives away evil and sorcery. It brings luck with legal issues.

Other Traditional Uses: Some buckthorn berries are toxic to ingest. This is a beloved firewood.

Chives

Scientific Name: *Allium schoenoprasum*

Color: Green

Color Extraction: Hapa zome is the best process for this plant. Also can be used to make plant imprints on Easter/Oestre eggs, as on page 169.

Plant: Sun

Myths and Meanings: Usefulness, love, healing

Healing Properties: Rich in vitamins C, K, and A. Supports immune health and memory function.

Magic: Breaking hexes, love magic. To break hexes, face north, cross the chives, and whisper your name. Now, you are free. To attract love, face south, cross the chives, and whisper the name of the one you love.

Other Traditional Uses: Used in soups, dips, and dishes with potato, seafood, or eggs.

Coyote Brush

Scientific Name: *Baccharis*

Colors: Yellows and browns

Color Extraction: Bring to a boil and then soak for at least two hours.

Plant: Full sun to partial shade

Myths and Meanings: Its fluffy white flowers, gone to seed, look like a coyote has brushed against the plant, leaving traces of its coat. Like coyotes, the plant symbolizes survival, adaptability, tenacity, resourcefulness, and cleverness.

Healing Properties: Traditionally, heated leaves were applied to the skin to reduce swelling. Teas from the leaves treated stomach issues.

Magic: Spells for protection, growth, and abundance. Shielding and shading.

Other Traditional Uses: Said to have been used to terminate pregnancy. Straight branches were used for making arrow shafts.

Crab Apple

Scientific Name: *Malus*

Colors: Pinks (apples); greens and browns (leaves)

Color Extraction: Place apples into boiling water and simmer for an hour. Leave to soak for two hours and then simmer for an hour more. Strain. Mordants may intensify color. Leaves can be eco-printed by being pressed into fabric and smashed, steamed, or frozen followed by thawing.

Plant: Sun

Myths and Meanings: Planted on graves to help the departed stay connected to nature in the afterlife. Greeks and Romans believed the tree brought fertility and immortality.

Healing Properties: Fruits are a good source of vitamin C. The blossoms are used in Ayurvedic medicine to treat gout and inflammation.

Magic: Banishes evil and supports powerful transformation when used in spell work.

Other Traditional Uses: Used to make jellies, juices, and wines.

Elder

Scientific Name: *Sambucus*

Colors: Pink that fades to beige (berry), beige (bark), mustard (leaves)

Color Extraction: Bark: soak for one week, and then simmer—do not boil—for one hour. Leaves: Pour boiling water over torn leaves. Soak overnight. Simmer for sixty minutes. Strain. Berries: Simmer until popped.

Plant: Sun

Myths and Meanings: Renewal and rebirth

Healing Properties: Elderberry syrup boosts the immune system against viruses: antioxidant, digestion aid, and anti-inflammatory properties.

Magic: Used for healing and breaking curses. To break a curse, anoint with elderberry oil.

Other Traditional Uses: Humans have worked with elderberries for healing since Neolithic times. Elder wood was used to create musical instruments and magic wands for ceremonies.

Eucalyptus

Scientific Name: *Eucalyptus*

Colors: Red, orange (*Eucalyptus cinerea*); brown (*Eucalyptus globulus*)

Color Extraction: Bring leaves to a low simmer—do not boil—for at least two hours.

Plant: Full sun to partial shade

Myths and Meanings: Tall and magical, eucalyptus represents the division of the Underworld, earth, and heaven.

Healing Properties: Added to balms and humidifiers, it can alleviate respiratory congestion and ease coughing. To lessen a baby's congestion, rub a poultice of crushed eucalyptus leaves on the bottoms of their feet. The leaves are also antibacterial and antifungal. They were used to sanitize cuts, cold sores, and athlete's foot. Tea can reduce fevers.

Magic: When inhaled, eucalyptus brings fresh energy, alleviates regrets and worries, and relieves mental exhaustion. It has short-lived, potent magic.

Other Traditional Uses: Eucalyptus essential oils are used to energize.

Fennel

Scientific Name: *Foeniculum vulgare*

Colors: Greens and yellows

Color Extraction: Cover with water and simmer. Strain. Works well for steam eco-printing (wrapping in fabric and steaming) or hapa zome (printing an impression of the plant by hammering or crushing, as described on page 123).

Plant: Sun

Myths and Meanings: Flattery and adultery. Prometheus used dry fennel stalks to carry the fire he stole from the gods.

Healing Properties: The seeds may induce menstruation.

Magic: Plant fennel around the house for protection. Hang fennel above the door and fill the locks with seeds to keep unwanted spirits away. Fennel candles will break streaks of bad luck.

Other Traditional Uses: All parts of the plant are edible. The bulb is often cooked, and the leaves are used to flavor salads and sauces.

Henna

Scientific Name: *Lawsonia inermis*

Colors: Brown, orange, and black

Color Extraction: Experts extract reddish-yellow henna dye from the leaves and stems of the tree by grinding them with slaked lime or lemon juice. Preprocessed henna powders are widely available for sale.

Plant: Full sun to partial shade

Myths and Meanings: Interconnectedness

Healing Properties: Cooling and antifungal properties

Magic: Increases receptiveness to natural energies. Carry henna on hikes to reconnect with nature.

Other Traditional Uses: Women across North Africa, Turkey, India, and the Arab world adorn their hands and feet with designs drawn from the natural world and local fabrics using henna.

Holy Basil/Tulsi

Scientific Name: *Ocimum sanctum*

Colors: Greenish-brown

Color Extraction: Print the leaves and stems using the hapa zome technique.

Plant: Sun

Meaning/Mythology: Queen of the herbs, sacred to the Hindu goddess Lakshmi.

Healing Properties: Also called the *Elixir of Life*, holy basil is important in Ayurvedic medicine. Usually, it is drunk as tea and supports the body during times of stress. It protects against viruses, helps stabilize metabolism and blood sugar, improves mood and neurological issues, improves blood pressure and cholesterol, and decreases inflammation.

Magic: Spreading the leaves in your home will keep it spiritually clear, drawing love, happiness, and systemic healing to you and your family. It will reduce conflict and arguments, adding sweetness to your life.

Other Traditional Uses: It can be used as a mouthwash, water purifier, and hand sanitizer.

Indigo (Fresh)

Scientific Name: *Indigofera*

Colors: Light blues, turquoise. A staple pigment plant of the ancient world.

Color Extraction: Traditionally dried and processed in a fermented bath to yield a deep purplish-blue, the fresh leaves can also be used immediately to create light blue and turquoise. Combine fresh leaves with a handful of ice and sprinkle salt on top. Knead the leaves with the salt and ice cubes. Use the liquid to dye or paint with. The flowers make a hot pink hapa zome print.

Plant: Full sun to partial shade

Myths and Meanings: Many cultures connect indigo to mystical realms, linking us with the unseen and divine.

Healing Properties: Used in traditional Chinese medicine to stimulate the immune system.

Magic: Indigo can be used in spells to help turn endings into new beginnings and failures into rebirths.

Other Traditional Uses: Focusing on cloth dyed with indigo while meditating will help unlock intuition and spiritual connection.

Ivy

Scientific name: *Hedera*

Colors: Yellows and greens

Color Extraction: Chop the leaves, cover them with water, and simmer for a few hours. Steep overnight and strain. It also can be eco-printed by being wrapped in fabric and steamed.

Plant: Full sun to partial shade

Myths and Meanings: Love and fidelity in Roman myths. Evergreen in ancient Egypt, ivy was dedicated to Osiris, who represented immortality. In India, it symbolizes wealth and prosperity.

Healing Properties: Ivy extract is said to help with warts.

Magic: Used in protection spells and New Year's divination. An ivy leaf is placed in a water bowl for twelve nights, usually during Christmas or Yule. A green leaf predicts good health. Place a leaf of ivy and a sprig of holly under the pillow to see a future lover's dreams. Carry a leaf of ivy to draw your future partner closer.

Other Traditional Uses: Ivy is unsafe to eat and an invasive plant in many places. Often, it is used for Yuletide decorations. Ivy was planted to cover walls to prevent witches from entering.

Japanese Maple

Scientific Name: *Acer palmatum*

Colors: Grays, beiges, and browns

Color Extraction: Boil leaves and bark for one hour. Strain and treat with mordants to shift color. Use the leaves for steam eco-printing and hapa zome.

Plant: Full sun to partial shade

Myths and Meanings: I am hesitating because I have concerns.

Healing Properties: Antioxidant and anti-inflammatory

Magic: Japanese maples are planted in front of homes to bring abundant blessings, peace, beauty, and patience.

Other Traditional Uses: Their edible leaves and seeds are used in traditional Japanese cuisine. Japanese maples also produce sap, which can be processed into syrup.

Juniper

Scientific Name: *Juniperus*

Colors: Tans

Color Extraction: Cover juniper cuttings with water and simmer for one hour. No mordant is needed for lightfastness.

Plant: Full sun

Myths and Meanings: Strength and wisdom

Healing Properties: Antioxidant, anticancer, anti-inflammatory, and antibacterial properties

Magic: Wear the berries in an amulet or add them to your bath to attract love. They are used in spells for luck, clarity, and wisdom.

Other Traditional Uses: Juniper is the flavoring agent in gin and can also be used for flavoring meats, sausage, and game. Juniper ash can be added to corn recipes, a tradition in the American Southwest.

Lemon Balm

Scientific Name: *Melissa officinalis*

Colors: Greens and browns

Color Extraction: Creates leaf prints using the hapa zome technique.

Plant: Sun

Myths and Meanings: My heart delights.

Healing Properties: Helps with colic. A calming herb that reduces anxiety, promotes sleep, and improves appetite. It helps ease discomfort from gas and indigestion.

Magic: Helps ease grief and dispel anxiety. If you are having difficulty, spend time with lemon balm. Its spirit will keep you company. Carry it with you so you can smell it throughout the day. Drink it in teas. Add it to your foods. Take lemon balm capsules at night with ashwagandha after ensuring they won't interact with your other medicines. Make a lemon balm spell cloth (page 18), printing the leaves onto something you wear.

Other Traditional Uses: Lemon balm is used to flavor foods and as an incense. It is a regular feature in medicinal gardens.

Loquat Leaves

Scientific Name: *Eriobotrya japonica*

Colors: Warm pinks

Color Extraction: Fill a saucepan with chopped leaves. Cover the mixture with water and simmer it for one hour. For best results, create a solar bath in a jar in the sun, keeping the leaves warm for at least a day. Adding alum may strengthen the color.

Plant: Sun

Myths and Meanings: In Chinese, they are called *làuhgwāt*, a "small tree related to the roses." They symbolize wealth, prosperity, and beauty.

Healing Properties: Antioxidant, anti-inflammatory, and analgesic

Magic: The leaves are used to enhance intuition and psychic abilities. Meditate with them to open the third eye and connect with the spiritual realm.

Other Traditional Uses: Loquats have a sweet, juicy, and delicate fruit.

Madder

Scientific Name: *Rubia tinctorum*

Colors: Red, vivid pink, or purple. A staple pigment plant of the ancient world.

Color Extraction: Madder root is red. It is considered mature after three years and most potent after five years. The roots can be pressed, smashed, or simmered to extract permanent color.

Plant: Full sun

Myths and Meanings: Calumny, false statements, or slander

Healing Properties: For dyeing only. Do not ingest madder. Although it was traditionally used for medicinal purposes and some websites advocate this, the risks associated with madder outweigh any benefits. The chemicals in madder may cause cancer and can lead to urine, saliva, sweat, tears, and breast milk turning red.

Magic: Used to dye wands and imbue them with deceptive power.

Other Traditional Uses: The Druids incorporated madder in girls' coming-of-age ceremonies.

Nettle

Scientific Name: *Urtica*

Other Name: *Mala mujer* (Spanish)

Color: Colorfast green dye

Color Extraction: Cover with boiling water and let sit overnight. Boil for one hour more.

Plant: Sun. Will tolerate some shade.

Myths and Meanings: Slander and pain. In Shakespeare, Ophelia holds nettles in her bouquet. Nettle can remind us how what was once painful can become part of our healing.

Healing Properties: Anti-inflammatory, antioxidant, analgesic, antiseptic, and supports heart health. Stinging nettle stings, but crushed nettle leaves can be made into a poultice to calm inflammation.

Magic: Carry a nettle satchel or sprinkle it around your home for protection. Plant it to ward off evil. Combine with yarrow in an amulet to help allay fears.

Other Traditional Uses: Young leaves can be cooked into curries and soups. Vikings burned nettle to prevent lightning strikes.

Oak Galls

Other Name: Oak apple

Colors: Black, gray, and purple. A staple pigment material of the ancient world.

Color Extraction: Please see the Oak Gall Ink recipe on page 139.

Plant: Oak trees in full sun: galls are formed by the gall wasp when it lays its eggs.

Myths and Meanings: Nature's ancient power

Healing Properties: Inside the gall is the pith. The sterile pith can be pressed against a small cut to disinfect and stop the bleeding.

Magic: Carried, added to a bath, or used as magical ink, oak galls dramatically increase the power of any spell.

Other Traditional Uses: Used for over 1,500 years, with the first recorded use of this ink dating back to the fourth century CE. *The Codex Sinaiticus*—the earliest complete Bible—was written in oak gall ink. Other early users included medieval royalty, Leonardo da Vinci, and early Americans when drafting the Constitution and Bill of Rights.

Oak Tree

Scientific Name: *Quercus*

Colors: Browns

Color Extraction: Cover oak leaves with boiling water and stew overnight. Add one inch more water and simmer gently for approximately one to two hours. Remove the water from heat when it has shifted to the desired color. Strain.

Plant: Full sun

Myths and Meanings: Strength. In Seneca legend, mighty oak stands with the evergreens, battling to hold on to his leaves, wearing down winter and helping to bring back spring.

Healing Properties: Oaks' inner bark is a potent astringent. Some healers grind it and brew it into a salve.

Magic: Oak leaves can be added to a bath to remove jinxes. When oak and mistletoe are burned together, the smoke causes unsettled spirits to leave. Oak wood is used for magic wands.

Other Traditional Uses: The Celts named the oak the King of Trees. Oak was used in rituals for strength and during Celtic holidays.

Peach (Leaves)

Scientific Name: *Prunus persica*

Colors: Yellow and green

Color Extraction: Fill your pot with leaves. Cover with water. Simmer for at least one hour. Adding alum will shift the color to bright yellow.

Plant: Sun

Myths and Meanings: Longevity, vitality, protection, love, wisdom, and fertility

Healing Properties: Rich in vitamin A, potassium, fluoride, and iron

Magic: Serve peaches to induce love. Branches are used to make divining rods and magical wands. Wearing a peach pit necklace wards off demons.

Other Traditional Uses: Beloved food from ancient China that traveled across Persia, Spain, and the Americas.

Pokeweed (Berries)

Scientific Name: *Phytolacca decandra*

Color: Magenta. A staple pigment plant of the ancient world.

Color Extraction: See Pokeberry Ink recipe on page 140.

Plant: Moist ground, sun, and some shade

Myths and Meanings: Courage

Healing Properties: Do not ingest. Poisonous unless processed meticulously.

Magic: Use this plant to make a powerful ink to write spells that break hexes. After hexes are broken, write another spell to bolster your courage.

Other Traditional Uses: Poisonous. The U.S. Declaration of Independence was first drafted in pokeberry ink. During the American Revolution, soldiers quickly made pokeberry juice from berries found in the wild for their letters.

Redwood Cones

Scientific Name: *Sequoia sempervirens*

Colors: Reds and browns

Color Extraction: Cover redwood cones with water in an aluminum pot and boil. Simmer for thirty minutes. Remove from heat and stew for several hours.

Plant: Full sun to shade. Will grow from seeds or bark.

Myths and Meanings: Strength, resilience, healing, and creating community

Healing Properties: New bright green needles are high in vitamin C. They have been used to treat head lice and hyperactivity and calm gums.

Magic: Their branches grow in a spiral resembling the Milky Way and DNA. Redwood trees connect the powers of heaven to earth. Under the redwoods, look up to recover spiritual belief and religious discipline, reuniting with nature.

Other Traditional Uses: The new growth, green tips can be substituted in recipes for baked goods that call for spices like sage and lavender. Redwood is used for furniture, home building, paddles, dugout canoes, and fishing tools. Redwood bark and root fibers are used in basketmaking.

Sagebrush

Scientific Name: *Artemisia tridentata*

Colors: Green, yellow, and gray

Color Extraction: Cover plants with water and soak overnight. Simmer for forty-five minutes. Use mordants to shift color.

Plant: Sun, semiarid and arid climates

Myths and Meanings: In the language of flowers: domestic virtue. Medieval herbalists believed sage plants flourish when all is well and wilt when something is not right.

Healing Properties: Antirheumatic, febrifuge (fever-reducer), ophthalmic (helping with eye ailments), and sedative. A decoction (reduction) of leaves treats the stomach and throat.

Magic: Sagebrush smoke purifies body and soul. Add to fires during rituals and use to smoke cleanse a structure's energy.

Other Traditional Uses: Fresh or dried, sage can be incorporated into savory dishes or drunk as tea. Sage is added to the smoke of the sweat lodge.

Sweet Gum

Scientific Name: *Liquidambar styraciflua*

Colors: Reds, purples, greens, and yellows

Color Extraction: Best by eco-printing dried and pressed leaves by wrapping them in fabric and steaming them.

Plant: Warm, temperate climate with a constant water source

Myths and Meanings: Unity. George Washington hoped this tree, which he believed to be unique to North America, would symbolize unity among the thirteen colonies. The European sweet gum tree is long extinct.

Healing Properties: Astringent, antimicrobial, and anti-inflammatory. Good for skin infections.

Magic: Sweet gum seedpods are called witch's burrs or witch balls and can be used as a powerful protection amulet.

Other Traditional Uses: The gum in the bark can create a resin to calm nerves. In 1519, Don Bernal Díaz del Castillo, who witnessed ceremonies between the Spanish conquistador Hernán Cortés and the Aztec leader Montezuma II, noted both drank an amber liquid from the sweet gum tree.

Thyme

Scientific Name: *Thymus vulgaris*

Colors: Browns

Color Extraction: Dry sprigs and grind them, or hapa zome, steeping, and freezing followed by thawing also work well.

Plant: Sun

Myths and Meanings: Courage, strength, and sacrifice

Healing Properties: Excellent in tonics for colds and coughs. Covering the chest with a thyme poultice and knocking on the breastbone will stimulate the thymus gland, which helps the body fight infection.

Magic: Good luck and protection from evil

Other Traditional Uses: Used to season meats, soups, seafood, and vegetables. It was also used to embalm corpses.

Toyon

Scientific Name: *Heteromeles arbutifolia*

Colors: Red, orange, and pinks

Color Extraction: Soak plant matter, including berries, leaves, and sticks, for a few days in the sun. Simmer for thirty minutes and soak again to enhance color—strain and shift color with mordants.

Plant: Sun, in well-drained soil. Drought tolerant.

Myths and Meanings: Fertility and new beginnings

Healing Properties: A tea from the leaves can be used as a stomach remedy.

Magic: Branches hung above doorways increase fertility and ward off evil spirits

Other Traditional Uses: The toyon pomes can be made into jelly. They can also be dried for later, cooked in porridge, or made into wine.

Tulip Tree (Leaves)

Scientific Name: *Liriodendron*

Colors: Browns and greens

Color Extraction: Use the leaves to create intricate prints with hapa zome.

Plant: Full sun, Mid-Atlantic to southern U.S.

Myths and Meanings: Luck and stability, and later, after the American Revolution, liberty

Healing Properties: Tulip tree bark contains salicylates used for pain relief. Tea from the bark can support digestion and restore health after stress. The inner bark of the root is thought to be most potent. Use the leaves to create a poultice for sores or scrapes.

Magic: The tulip tree is ancient, and its seedpod retains the qualities of prehistory. Use them to build spells that create bridges connecting us with our distant ancestors of all species.

Other Traditional Uses: Tulip tree wood is used to create musical instruments, floorboards, boxes, bowls, baskets, and carvings.

Wild Buckwheat

Scientific Name: *Polygonum convolvulus*

Color: Reddish-brown

Color Extraction: Collect the flowers and cover them with boiling water. Steep until the desired color is achieved. Strain.

Plant: Sun. It prefers disturbed soils, agricultural land, and landscaped areas.

Myths and Meanings: In Korean traditions, buckwheat flowers signify the arrival of a lover.

Healing Properties: A tea made from boiled flowers or leaves can be used as an eyewash or a mouthwash. A remedy for headaches, stomachaches, and bladder infections.

Magic: Use in charms and spells for money and protection. It helps with fasting when worn.

Other Traditional Uses: Edible when prepared correctly to make tea and flour from the husks.

Willow

Scientific Name: *Salix*

Colors: Beiges

Color Extraction: No mordant is needed. Cover leaves and bark with water. Soak for a few days and then simmer for thirty minutes. Using just bark yields a warmer beige.

Plant: Sun, near the water in cool and temperate climates

Myths and Meanings: The willow helps us integrate change into our lives. It reminds us to find inspiration in small things, even in the shadow of death. In Celtic myth, the willow fairies like to leave their tree at night and follow travelers, whispering and muttering, frightening them.

Healing Properties: Only for those who are not allergic to aspirin. Willow bark contains salicylic acid used for pain relief, acne treatments, headaches, and other inflammatory ailments. Brew willow bark teas or chew the bark to relieve pain and inflammation. Make a willow bark poultice to relieve psoriasis, rosacea, acne, and dandruff.

Magic: Wand-making. To create a willow love knot spell, braid three branches together. Tie the braid into a loose circle and keep it by your bed. Place the name or picture of the person you love inside the circle.

Other Traditional Uses: All willows are edible, but some are not palatable. Willow leaves are incredibly high in vitamin C. The inner bark is a good source of calcium, magnesium, and zinc.

Woad (Fresh Leaves)

Scientific Name: *Isatis tinctoria*

Colors: Blue, gray, turquoise, and beige. A staple pigment plant of the ancient world.

Color Extraction: Traditionally, woad was processed with urine and fermented. With fresh leaves, cover with ice. Knead the leaves and ice cubes. Use the liquid to paint or dye.

Plant: Sun. Note: Woad is considered invasive in Arizona, California, Colorado, Idaho, Montana, Nevada, New Mexico, Oregon, Utah, Washington, and Wyoming.

Myths and Meanings: In North Africa, woad symbolized nobility and elegance. In Victorian England, it meant "looking forward to our next encounter, and continuing our relationship in good health." Woad is said to be the offering preferred by Pictish ancestors.

Healing Properties: The woad plant's roots are used in traditional Chinese medicine to make a *banlangen*, thought to be anti-inflammatory and stop bleeding.

Magic: Used in defensive magic spells. Wear for protection and employ for banishing.

Other Traditional Uses: Woad can be a bug repellent. Ancient Egyptians used it to dye the cloth wrappings applied for the mummies. Celtic warriors were said to paint their bodies with blue woad dye before riding into battle. The woad may have helped treat their wounds.

KITCHEN GRIMOIRE

Kitchen Table Magic

Plant-based diets are excellent for our health, and they are a great choice to make for the earth. Eating plants reduces our consumption of foods that release lots of carbon into the atmosphere.

Unfortunately, not everyone wants to eat plants—or elaborate food. Cooked vegetables are sometimes off-putting for young ones and induce sensory suffering for the squeamish. Others want everything as oniony, garlicky, and spicy as possible, with lots of textures and variety.

Plants allow us to make one dish appeal to a range of palates. For example, a simple platter of nachos at my house could have one end that is just chips and cheese (for the food avoidant); a stripe that is just chips, beans, and cheese (for the young and picky); a stripe that incorporates tomatoes, onions, and chili peppers (for me); and then a stripe with as many chilis and onions as the chips can hold (for my husband, who grew up eating kimchi with every meal). A spectrum!

The finicky can eat their veggies on the side, and they often prefer them raw—a veggie plate with every meal. A simple rainbow can please and nourish the pickiest of eaters: the sweet orange snap of carrot sticks, light green watery celery strings, purple twists of cabbage, and fruits like dark green crunchy cucumber, red juicy bell pepper, and the sweet-tart of blueberries. Each speaks the plant language of color, expressing which nutrients they offer.

It's perfect! Simple. And it turns out these raw plant foods contain more vitamins than cooked vegetables. Healthy, easy, and climate-friendly beat fancy.

Now, that's some kitchen table magic.

Magical Relationships

So, besides being acceptable to picky children, what else makes this food magical?

Plant magic comes from connection. My mother's greens recipe, in which she carefully cut away the center stems and rolled the leaves in cinnamon like cigars, connected us to our ancestors, even after the amnesia of assimilation. On the other side of my family, my grandmother's lentil soup recipe, full of rice and bones, invoked a landscape our family was forced to leave quickly.

I hold a strawberry, fresh from the store or a farmers market, and reflect on the many hands that cared for this fragile fruit, nurturing and protecting it since it was a seed. We have a special relationship with an herb harvested from a garden in the yard or a flowerpot in the apartment window. I care for the herb, rejoicing in its growth, and it nourishes me with beauty and nutrients.

These kinds of relationships—this loving interconnectedness—are the heart of nature's magic.

Plant magic begins when we shift our awareness. We may learn a plant's history and realize that we are connected to its journey from places far and near when we ingest it. Perhaps this plant's ancestors traveled across the same countries as ours did.

*As you prepare a meal, whether you are snapping
a piece of vibrant carrot or slicing a fragrant lemon,
make an offering to honor your ancestors.
They are with you.*

To Express Gratitude for Your Meal

Offerings: Candle, a bowl of water, an altar. Or simply, gratitude and attention.

Blessings before a meal: (choose which resonates)
With this offering, we thank:

Deities: *We thank the loving spirit of (your choosing) for our meal and all our blessings.*

Food: *We are thankful for our food. We share this earth with animals and plants whose ancestors are connected to ours.*

Who carried the food: *We are thankful for those who gathered, carried, and prepared our food. May they be blessed.*

Ancestors: *We are thankful to our ancestors for their journeys that bring us together to share this meal. May they continue to watch over us.*

Toast: To our adventure.

Perhaps our ancestors had a traditional relationship with a plant we prepare in our kitchen. An edible plant's magic will shimmer for us once we learn how practitioners have used it since ancient times. Plants' connections to the fifth element support transformation. If we give them attention, those powers grow more vital within our bodies and homes.

From Scraps to Spells

Another way we can help the earth is to reduce our food waste. One method to do this is to collect kitchen scraps and turn them into magic spells, art projects, and medicine. What's left can become compost and then part of the soil again, ready to nourish new life.

Children like to investigate the cupboard in my studio. It's mystifying to them that a grown-up has a drawers of onion skins, avocado pits, and expired dry black beans. My oldest explains that I act like "three kids in a trench coat."

After cooking, I save useful scraps, making sure they are dry before storing them. The onion skins will become a dye for Oestre. The pits will be made into ink for love letters, and the black beans create the loveliest blue paint wash for protective spells. This kind of experimentation likely resonates with children because it is playful. *Play* is trying to figure out the world using creativity.

In this chapter, we will play with our food.

Plants support health, wisdom, and love—
the magical recipe for nurturing.

Vegetables, Fruits, and More Catalog

Annatto

Scientific Name: *Bixa orellana*

Other Names: *Bixa* (Taino), *achiotl* (Nahuatl)

Origin: Northern South America and Central America

Colors: Red, orange

Color Extraction: Soak the seeds in olive oil or grind them and use them as a pigment. Mix with wintergreen or thyme extract to prevent mold.

Plant: Sun

Myths and Meanings: Annatto comes from the seeds of the achiote tree, associated with masculinity and the sun. The achiote tree is featured in the Tupi flood myth. In it, a warrior saves himself by climbing this tree, while the peaceful man saves himself by climbing the gentle genipa palm tree.

Healing Properties: Annatto is used to treat burns and skin infections. It fights viruses and supports the digestive system. It helps to balance blood sugar and to treat fevers.

Magic: Annatto wards off evil and disease. The seeds can support the formulation of prophecy. Light a candle. Dip a hawthorn stick into annatto extract and use it to do automatic writing or drawing. To ensure the prediction comes true, place it where you can see it daily.

Other Traditional Uses: Used for writing Mayan manuscripts and as body paint, annatto is a main ingredient in Sazón seasoning and is used as a natural food coloring. It is also used as an insect repellent and in cosmetics.

Avocado

Scientific Name: *Persea americana*

Other Name: *Āhuacatl* (Nahuatl)

Origin: Mexico and Central America

Colors: Pinks, maroons, and reddish-browns

Color Extraction: Cover skins with water and heat to a simmer for an hour. (Do not boil.) Soak overnight and reheat for thirty minutes. Strain. Boil pits for thirty minutes with soda ash. Longer boiling will deepen the color. Use soy milk as a mordant.

Using an aluminum dye pot will brighten the color of the bath.

Plant: Sun

Myths and Meanings: Because the flower shifts from male to female, it can symbolize gender fluidity. Aztecs called it *āhuacatl*, meaning "testicle."

Healing Properties: A source of healthy fats, vitamins, and minerals, avocado supports immune health and the circulatory system. Facial and anti-aging skin treatments often contain avocado. Avocado softens and makes hair shinier.

Magic: Used in spells for beauty and relaxation. Serve it to a love interest to put them at ease. Plant the pit, and when it sprouts, it will increase your physical attraction.

Other Traditional Uses: Considered a superfood, avocados are used in dishes that are traditional to the Western Hemisphere and beloved worldwide. The skins contain tannins and can be used as a mordant in dye baths. Avocados are depicted in 10,000-year-old paintings from Coxcatlán, Mexico.

Beet

Scientific Name: *Beta vulgaris*

Origin: The shores of the Mediterranean connecting Europe, the Middle East, and North Africa

Colors: Red, magenta, and gold

Color Extraction: Cover chopped beets with one part vinegar to two parts water and simmer. Strain. If dyeing, set color with heat. Leaves make beautiful hapa zome.

Plant: Sun

Myths and Meanings: Passion, love, and beauty, connected to Aphrodite

Healing Properties: Antioxidant, anti-inflammatory, high in nutrients and fiber. Not for those experiencing kidney stones.

Magic: To enhance your connection, write about the one you love in beetroot juice.

Other Traditional Uses: Steamed, roasted, used in salads and borscht. Beet greens are edible and nutritious, cooked or raw. The roots are used to dye fabrics and Easter/Oestre eggs.

Black Beans

Scientific Name: *Phaseolus vulgaris*

Origin: Southern Mexico and Central America

Colors: Blue and indigo

Color Extraction: A use for expired dry beans—place dry beans in a jar. Cover with boiling water and steep for one hour. Strain.

Plant: Sun

Myths and Meanings: In ancient Rome, people performed rites to protect themselves from the unburied dead and other threats from the Otherworld during the Lemuria Festival. During the festival, they tossed dark beans to ward off evil spirits. The spirits were thought to follow the beans, leaving the mortals safe.

Healing Properties: Packed with disease-fighting antioxidants, they have anti-inflammatory properties and are a good source of fiber, iron, and protein.

Magic: Carried raw in a pouch or eaten, black beans help us overcome obstacles and make challenging decisions.

Other Traditional Uses: Black beans are a low-calorie, nutrient-dense food.

Black Tea

Scientific Name: *Camellia sinensis*

Origin: Assam district of India

Colors: Browns and tans

Color Extraction: Steep tea in boiling water, adding more tea leaves to darken. For each cup of steeping tea, stir in one teaspoon of gum arabic and one tablespoon of vinegar. Simmer for thirty minutes. Cool.

Plant: Sun

Myths and Meanings: Strength, courage, wealth, willpower, energy, and alertness

Healing Properties: Antioxidant. It supports heart health and is anti-inflammatory.

Magic: Lends strength as you take steps toward happiness. Visualize your desired future as you drink black tea, and your dreams will come true.

Other Traditional Uses: Drunk to increase focus, relieve headaches, and awaken. Black tea with bergamot (Earl Grey tea) can be carried to draw wealth.

Blackberry

Scientific Name: *Rubus*

Origin: Western and Central Europe and North Africa, Asia, and the Americas

Colors: Purples and magenta

Color Extraction: Crush and strain berries. Add one teaspoon of vinegar and one teaspoon of salt. Berry inks are impermanent. Blackberry leaves make beautiful hapa zome.

Plant: Sun

Myths and Meanings: Blackberry symbolizes remorse in Europe's language of flowers. In Hebrew, the blackberry signifies God's voice and divine love of humanity. The burning bush in the Old Testament may have been a blackberry bush.

Healing Properties: Antioxidant, anti-inflammatory, high in fiber and nutrients. It is a good source of vitamin C and immune system support. A tea made of blackberry leaves soothes the throat.

Magic: Blackberry leaves and berries support healing and attract material success. Shared as a couple, they can increase pleasure and protect deep bonds. After an argument, write a love letter in blackberry juice and plant it in the ground so that your love will grow. Gather blackberries under the waxing gibbous moon to protect against evil runes or curses.

Other Traditional Uses: Blackberry roots make strong twine. In North America, the thorny bushes were used as barricades for gardens and villages.

Bok Choy

Scientific Name: *Brassica rapa*

Other Name: *Qin cai* (Mandarin Chinese)

Origin: Yangtze River Delta, China

Colors: Green, yellow, and brown

Color Extraction: Make leaf prints using the hapa zome technique.

Plant: Sun

Myths and Meanings: In Hong Kong, it means "100 kinds of wealth and prosperity."

Healing Properties: Packed with nutrients and antioxidants, bok choy supports the immune system. It is an excellent source of quercetin that can help reduce inflammation and fight viruses when taken with zinc.

Magic: Draws prosperity and supports healing. Cook with bok choy the evening before an event that could impact you financially. Make soups with bok choy to protect your health, stirring in healing intentions.

Other Traditional Uses: Statues of bok choy can be placed in the home to draw wealth and prosperity.

Caraway

Scientific Name: *Carum carvi*

Origin: Anatolia

Colors: Tans

Color Extraction: Brew like tea to create a staining color using one teaspoon of seeds per cup of water.

Plant: Sun

Myths and Meanings: Faithfulness. Believed to be most powerful when collected during the feast of St. John the Baptist.

Healing Properties: Chewing the seeds after meals helps digestion by relieving gas and soothing the stomach. Supports blood circulation.

Magic: Caraway's magic keeps loved things close and repels what is unwanted. Traditionally tucked into purses and wallets, caraway prevents objects from being stolen. Caraway seeds are mixed into domestic animal feed to keep them close and prevent them from getting lost. Chewing caraway seeds before kissing will make someone love you more. Artists chew caraway seeds to keep their muses close. Placed under cribs and on top of coffins, caraway seeds repel evil spirits, thieves, and curses.

Other Traditional Uses: Wonderful for gardens, caraway draws predator pollinators. The taproot can be roasted and eaten. Used in liqueurs and to flavor sauerkraut.

Carrot

Scientific Name: *Daucus carota*

Origin: Afghanistan

Colors: Orange or purples, depending on the carrot's color (peels), greens (leaves)

Color Extraction: Cover carrot peels with water. Add a half cup of salt and two cups of white vinegar for every eight cups of water. Bring the pot to a simmer and let it steep for two hours. If using as a dye, dry fabric in the dryer to set.

Plant: Sun in well-drained soil

Myths and Meanings: Wild carrot flowers mean "sanctuary." The ancient Greeks used them for love potions.

Healing Properties: Carrots have lots of vitamin A, which benefits the eyes. Full of antioxidants, carrots can also help settle the stomach.

Magic: Carrots support fertility and passion. Share carrot soup with a partner to inspire love and lust.

Other Traditional Uses: In medieval times, carrots were used to treat syphilis and animal bites.

Cherry

Scientific Name: *Prunus cerasus*

Origin: Anatolia

Colors: Pinks (fruit); yellow and green (leaves)

Color Extraction: Fruit: Simmer the whole fruits in water until they pop. Let steep for three hours. Strain. Leaves: Cover with water and simmer for one hour.

Plant: Sun

Myths and Meanings: Renewal and optimism. Cherry blossoms welcome spring while reminding us of the temporary nature of being.

Healing Properties: Anti-inflammatory cherries contain vitamins C, A, and K. Cherries may help with gout and sleep troubles.

Magic: To attract love, tie a strand of your hair to a branch of cherry blossoms or add them to your bath.

Other Traditional Uses: Cherry wood is used to make bagpipes and furniture. Having cherry wood in the home will draw happiness.

Cinnamon

Scientific Name: *Cinnamomum verum*

Origin: Sri Lanka

Color: Reddish-brown

Color Extraction: Combine cinnamon and honey to create a healthy hair dye. Mix cinnamon with paint to give colors a rusty look.

Plant: Sun, humidity

Myths and Meanings: My fortune is yours.

Healing Properties: Rich in antioxidants and anti-inflammatory, cinnamon supports heart health and balances metabolism. Bringing cinnamon into your diet helps regulate blood sugar. Add cinnamon

105

to bath salts to treat congestion. Combine with some eucalyptus to increase the bath's effectiveness.

Magic: Abundance, wealth, riches, money, prosperity. Sprinkle cinnamon on the threshold to attract prosperity to your home. Place a cinnamon broom upside down behind your front door to inspire house guests to leave quickly.

Other Traditional Uses: Imported to Egypt as early as 2000 BCE, cinnamon was used as part of the embalming process.

Citrus

Scientific Name: *Citrus*

Origin: Northeast India, Southwestern China, Myanmar, Fiji, Vanuatu, Solomon Islands, and Papua New Guinea

Colors: Yellows, golds, and greens

Color Extraction: Cover peels with water and simmer for fifteen to twenty minutes. Strain. Alum and other mordants will shift the color.

Plant: Sun

Myths and Meanings: Across Asia and the Middle East, citrus blossoms mean purity and innocence.

Healing Properties: Citrus is anti-inflammatory and high in vitamin C, calcium, and fiber. Supports the immune system; lowers blood pressure and cholesterol.

Magic: Good luck, cleansing, and purification come from interacting with citrus. For winter rituals, pierce the skin of an orange with cloves, creating a pomander for good luck, health, and protection. Citrus will enhance focus and support a shift of perspective to a fresh point of view.

Other Traditional Uses: In Chinese culture, oranges are given during the Lunar New Year to bring good fortune and abundance. Sailors used citrus to prevent scurvy, "the scourge of the seas." Make a calming tea with dried orange leaves.

Chili Pepper

Scientific Name: *Capsicum annuum*

Other Name: *Chīlli* (Nahuatl)

Origin: Lowlands of Brazil; some argue they come from all over the Western Hemisphere.

Colors: Reds and greens

Color Extraction: Cover with one part vinegar to three parts water and simmer for one hour. Strain.

Plant: Sun

Myths and Meanings: Fertility, luck, and resistance

Healing Properties: Chili stimulates digestion, speeds metabolism, and reduces obesity. It supports heart health and is anti-inflammatory. Mayans used chilis to treat the lungs and throat. The Aztecs used it to lift the mood.

Magic: In the Western Hemisphere, chili is used for fertility and sex spells. Chili is used in cooking and charms to prevent gossip and ward off jealousy. The Incas prohibited the use of chilis at initiation and funeral rites. Chili is used to cast hexes.

Other Traditional Uses: Chilis hung in the window are a bug repellent. Gardeners plant them to keep pests away.

Cloves

Scientific Name: *Syzygium aromaticum*

Origin: Indonesia and India

Colors: Tans and browns

Color Extraction: Add whole cloves to boiling water. Simmer for one hour. Let steep overnight. Strain.

Plant: Sun

Myths and Meanings: Guardian who wards off negative energy

Healing Properties: Antioxidant, antibacterial, anti-inflammatory. Highly diluted clove essential oil has traditionally been used to soothe tooth pain. Create a clove tincture by following the process on page 180.

Magic: Banishing, healing, love, and money. Add cloves to charge any spell with more energy. For banishing spells, boil thirteen cloves for thirteen minutes and visualize yourself free of whoever is causing you trouble. Now, withdraw your attention from them for thirteen days.

Other Traditional Uses: Cloves can be used as a preservative to prevent molding of natural pigments.

Coffee

Scientific Name: *Coffea*

Other Name: *Cafēnyōlli* (Nahuatl)

Origin: Ethiopia

Colors: Browns

Color Extraction: Grind beans and pour boiling water through them. For darker colors, submerge ground beans in boiling water until the desired color is achieved. Strain.

Plant: Sun

Myths and Meanings: Hope, rebirth, new beginnings

Healing Properties: Antioxidant, supports heart health and weight management, and can relieve pain. Impacts mental health.

Magic: Coffee helps us focus our intentions and dispel nightmares. Place whole beans on your altar. Seeing coffee flowers when feeling troubled shifts your perceptions and inspires hope.

Other Traditional Uses: Coffee grounds can be used to repel insects and fertilize the garden and are seen as a gift from Allah by the Sufis, who perpetuated its use.

Collard Greens

Scientific Name: *Collard*

Origin: Eastern Mediterranean

Colors: Green and beige

Color Extraction: Brewed like tea, the leaves create a beige dye. For best results, use the hapa zome process.

Plant: Sun

Myths and Meanings: Hope for the future

Healing Properties: Vitamin K supports bone health and liver function. Collard greens are rich in vitamins A, C, E, and B6 and dietary fiber, which supports digestion.

Magic: Collards draw wealth and good fortune when eaten.

Other Traditional Uses: Collard greens are traditionally eaten with black-eyed peas and corn bread at the start of the new year for prosperity.

Cranberry

Scientific Name: *Vaccinium*

Origin: Great Britain and eastern mountains of North America

Colors: Pinks

Color Extraction: Cover cranberries with water. Simmer for fifteen minutes. Crush the berries and simmer for fifteen more minutes. Strain.

Plant: Sun, in a marsh

Myths and Meanings: Cure for heartache

Healing Properties: Drinking cranberry juice or extract prevents urinary tract infections and ulcers and can relieve pain when urinating. Cranberries are full of antioxidants and support the immune system, heart, and liver health.

Magic: Vitality, energy, healing, love, and protection. Add cranberries to a spell jar at the beginning of the year to help you feel protected as you begin anew. To complete the spell, gather other objects that call to you. They will help you. Focus on your jar when you need a boost of energy.

Other Traditional Uses: Cranberries are often part of Samhain and Yule celebrations, strung with orange to create vibrant decorations that bring positive energy to celebrations.

Garlic

Scientific Name: *Allium sativum*

Origin: South Asia, Central Asia, and northeastern Iran

Colors: Purples (flower and some skins) and green (leaves)

Color Extraction: Hapa zome and eco-printing by steaming, steeping, and freezing followed by thawing work well.

Plant: Sun

Myths and Meanings: Good luck and protected prosperity. Thought to repel vampires.

Healing Properties: Antibacterial, antifungal, antiviral, and antioxidant. Supports the immune system and all aspects of physical health.

Magic: Protects prosperity by repelling thieves and parasitic personalities. Garlic blesses the home when planted near windows and entrances.

Other Traditional Uses: Used as an insect repellent and for deworming. In medieval Europe, priests wore garlic masks to protect against the bubonic plague.

Mint

Scientific Name: *Mentha*

Origin: Europe, Asia, Australia

Color: Green

Color Extraction: Hapa zome

Myths and Meanings: Virtue

Plant: Sun. Thrives in cold weather.

Healing Properties: Calm stomachs. Cooling for the throat and skin. Balances calming teas.

Magic: Used in spells or carried for protection, healing, and attracting money. Pluck a mint leaf from the snow to change your fortune.

Other Traditional Uses: Used in ice cream, teas, and sweets.

Onion

Scientific Name: *Allium cepa*

Origin: Iran, Pakistan, Central Asia

Colors: Oranges, golds, greens, and reds

Color Extraction: Cover skins with water or one part vinegar to three parts water. Simmer until the color leaches out. Soak overnight to deepen the color. An excellent egg dye for Easter/Oestre. Adding mordants will shift the colors.

Plant: Sun

Myths and Meanings: Patience, good fortune, prosperity and unity

Healing Properties: Onions contain antioxidants and are antiseptic and anti-inflammatory. They contribute to preventing heart disease and improving bone density. High in fiber, they support healthy digestion.

Magic: Ancient Egyptians treasured the onion, believing its layers were a diagram of time and the universe. Believing the onion could absorb negative energies and impurities, they would place onions in the eye sockets of the deceased.

Other Traditional Uses: Anglo-Saxons ate onions and sages to aid digestion when consuming rich foods. Russians used onion poultices in World War II to disinfect wounds.

Plum

Scientific Name: *Prunus domestica*

Origin: China

Colors: Yellow and green (leaves); blue to purple (black plum skin)

Color Extraction: Yellows and greens: Cover the leaves with water and simmer for at least two hours. Soak overnight. Use mordants to shift the tones. Blue to purple: Collect black plum skins. Add three cups of water for every one cup of skins. Boil and simmer for five minutes. Remove from heat. Let stand for thirty minutes and check the color. Stew longer if necessary.

Plant: Sun

Myths and Meanings: In China, plum blossoms mean perseverance and hope because they mark the earth's awakening from winter to spring.

Healing Properties: Nutrient-rich with vitamins C, A, and K. Benefits digestion. Antioxidant.

Magic: Serve plums to the ones you love, and they will be attracted to you. Plums are an aphrodisiac. Eat plums with your lover to enhance intimacy. Carry their stones when you are apart to increase your spiritual connection.

Other Traditional Uses: The Egyptians and Greeks ate plums to relax the mind and the body.

Pomegranate

Scientific Name: *Punica granatum*

Origin: Iran and Afghanistan

Colors: Magenta (seeds); yellows, greens, and grays (skins)

Color Extraction: Soak the rind in hot water overnight. Simmer for one hour. Shift the color to gray using iron; other mordants may bring out greens.

Plant: Sun

Myths and Meanings: Prosperity, hope, and abundance. When Persephone entered the Underworld, she was instructed not to eat or she could never leave. Persephone ate six pomegranate seeds, and so Hades, the god of the dead, would not let her return to the surface. He made her his queen. Persephone's mother, Demeter, goddess of the harvest, missed her daughter so much that she threw the world into endless winter. Zeus struck a bargain between Demeter and Hades so that Persephone could return to the surface for six months each year. When Persephone is here, the world thaws, seeds grow into crops, and harvest is successful. When she is gone, the world goes dormant until her return.

Healing Properties: Astringent and antioxidant. Supports digestive, immune system, heart, and urinary health. It may increase endurance.

Magic: Associated with the spirit world. To increase your connection to your ancestors, use pomegranate juice as an ink to write to them, or when thinking about them, add pomegranate juice or seeds to a tea. Place a whole fruit on your ancestor's altar as an offering.

Other Traditional Uses: The skin can be used as a mordant when dyeing fabric. It is one of the oldest fruits cultivated by humans. Used in carpet dyes in the ancient world.

Prickly Pear Cactus/Nopal

Scientific Name: *Opuntia*

Other Name: *Nochtli* (Nahuatl)

Origin: North, Central, and South America

Color: Magenta

Color Extraction: The fruit's pigment is similar to a beet's. Crush or juice the fruit to create pigments.

Plant: Sun, arid, sandy soil. Will grow from cuttings.

Myths and Meanings: Motherly love. The life-giving plant. Because it

nourishes even though it lives in the desert, it is revered for its vitality and appears in many traditional indigenous stories and myths.

Healing Properties: Balances blood sugar, preventing diabetes, obesity, and hangovers. Anti-inflammatory, antiviral, antifungal, antibacterial.

Magic: Protects against enemies, both spiritual and physical. Have a cactus at each corner of your house. Potted cacti absorb negative energy, releasing it when you replant them each year.

Other Traditional Uses: Made into jellies and candies.

Red Cabbage

Scientific Name: *Brassica oleracea var. capitata f. rubra*

Origin: Mediterranean regions of Europe

Colors: Blues, pinks, and purples

Color Extraction: A more temporary dye, best used for Easter/Oestre eggs.

Plant: Sun

Myths and Meanings: Moon mysticism. After harvesting the cabbagehead, mark the stalk with an *x* to protect it from the fairies so it can continue growing greens.

Healing Properties: Nursing mothers place cabbage leaves on their breasts to relieve pain and clogged milk ducts. Wrap the neck with cabbage leaves to relieve an inflamed throat.

Magic: Cabbage brings us closer to sensing the interconnectedness of life and essential truths. The couple who eats cabbage stew on their wedding night will soon be blessed with a stable marriage and a pregnancy.

Other Traditional Uses: Cabbage was the only internal remedy used by ancient Romans for 600 years. They would seal oaths by swearing on the cabbage.

Rhubarb

Scientific Name: *Rheum rhabarbarum*

Origin: China, Mongolia, and Siberia

Colors: Lightfast yellow and orange (roots)

Color Extraction: Harvest by dividing to preserve the plants. Chop up right after harvesting. Cover with water and simmer for thirty minutes. Soak overnight. Strain.

Plant: Sun in well-drained, poor, sandy soil

Myths and Meanings: Good advice

Healing Properties: Anti-inflammatory. A good source of antioxidants and vitamin K. Supports bone health and blood-clotting. Used in Chinese medicine to cure digestive problems.

Magic: Rhubarb protects love. Use in spells for fidelity, the male libido, and to protect from disease. The tangy roots are often combined with strawberries to make pies. Strawberry rhubarb pie is, itself, a love spell. Harvested at the opposite ends of the moon cycle, the strawberry combines feminine energy with masculine rhubarb.

Other Traditional Uses: Full of tannins, rhubarb leaves can be used as a mordant for dyes.

Rosemary

Scientific Name: *Rosmarinus officinalis*

Origin: Hills by the Mediterranean and on the Iberian Peninsula

Colors: Browns, green, and purple

Color Extraction: Hapa zome and eco-printing by steaming, steeping, and freezing followed by thawing work well.

Plant: Sun, sandy soil

Myths and Meanings: Dew of the sea. Aphrodite was said to have emerged from the sea draped in rosemary.

Healing Properties: Used in brain tonics to improve function and memory. Aids in digestion. Rosemary poultices can reduce inflammation. Rosemary's essential oil can act as a stimulant to increase physical activity in children; rub rosemary on the bottoms of their feet.

Magic: Used in spells to enhance memory—including of past lives—and psychic cleansing. Crush rosemary sprigs and inhale their scent as you meditate or walk in nature. Cleaning magic tools with rosemary smoke purifies while enhancing memories of past spells.

Other Traditional Uses: Sewn into pillows to banish nightmares.

Spinach

Scientific Name: *Spinacia oleracea*

Origin: Iran

Colors: Greens

Color Extraction: Chop spinach and cover every one cup with two cups of water in a blender. Liquify. Strain and add one teaspoon of salt to every cup of spinach. Alternative: Add one cup of spinach to two cups of water to a saucepan. Simmer for one hour. Let the bath cool and strain.

Plant: Sun

Myths and Meanings: Passion, fertility, and strength

Healing Properties: Spinach is rich in iron, vitamins C and E, potassium, and magnesium. An excellent source of protein, spinach helps regulate blood sugar levels and increases bone density. It supports the immune and digestive systems and heart health and prevents disease.

Magic: Spinach brings the strength and positive energy to persist and endure, helping you reach your goals. Eat a spinach dish to help yourself connect to your inner child. Write your intentions in spinach ink and plant the paper in the ground so they can grow.

Other Traditional Uses: Thought to help children grow and recover from illness.

Star Anise

Scientific Name: *Illicium verum*

Origin: Mediterranean and Western Asia

Colors: Browns and tans

Color Extraction: Color can be extracted from the leaves, roots, or herb in dry powder form. Cover with water, simmer for one hour, and then soak overnight. Strain. Use mordants to shift colors and add permanence.

Plant: Sun

Myths and Meanings: Psychic abilities, connection to the spiritual world

Healing Properties: Star anise has antioxidant, antimicrobial, antifungal, anti-inflammatory, and sedative properties. Chinese star anise is used in cooking and herbal remedies. Japanese star anise is toxic.

Magic: Star anise enhances clarity of thought and psychic abilities. Use star anise to connect to the fifth element in divination spells and satchels for astral travel.

Other Traditional Uses: Focus on star anise during meditation to shift to a positive mindset.

Tomato

Scientific Name: *Solanum lycopersicum*

Other Name: *Tomatl* (Nahuatl)

Origin: Mexico, South and Central America

Colors: Reds and pinks

Color Extraction: Cover tomatoes with water. Simmer for fifteen minutes. Crush and simmer for fifteen more minutes. Strain the mixture. Or steam tomatoes and then blend.

Plant: Sun, with companion plants like marigold and basil

Myths and Meanings: After cultivation, the Aztecs called tomatoes *xitomatl*, meaning "plump with navel" or "fat water with navel," perhaps alluding to the tomato's connection to pregnancy and the creation of new life.

Healing Properties: Tomatoes are full of antioxidants. They help lower blood pressure and cholesterol. They have antibacterial, anti-inflammatory, and antiviral properties. They may also lower the chances of stroke.

Magic: Tomatoes are full of creative energy. They are used for aphrodisiac spells or rituals to enhance creativity. Save tomato seeds for spell work or to place on your altar. Planting tomato seeds is a spell that brings creative energy to the home.

Other Traditional Uses: Tomatoes have been used to create poultices to help with sunburns.

Turmeric

Scientific Name: *Curcuma longa*

Origin: Southern India and Indonesia

Colors: Yellows

Color Extraction: Bring eight cups of water to a simmer. Add one-quarter to three-quarters of a cup of turmeric. Add more to make the color more intense. Simmer for ten minutes. Let stand for one hour.

Plant: Sun. Will grow from tuber.

Myths and Meanings: The hidden meaning of songs. Turmeric also represents purity and our spiritual connection with the earth.

Healing Properties: A powerful anti-inflammatory, turmeric balances blood sugar, supports cardiovascular health, and improves liver function. Wrap arthritic joints with a turmeric poultice for warmth.

Magic: Connected to the Divine Mother, turmeric is used in purification, protection, and abundance rituals in many cultures. Its smell drives away angry spirits. Use turmeric for spells for healing, strength, and vitality. Create a turmeric color bath. Soak a piece of paper, and while it is still wet, drip the color onto the paper. As you watch the color spread, breathe to the solar plexus five times, focusing on the color. This will help you heal and hear your intuitive responses about what will come. You can use this color bath to dye fabric for your altar.

Other Traditional Uses: In some cultures, turmeric is used as a sacred anointment for couples who are about to be married, new babies, and the dead.

Walnut

Scientific Name: *Juglans regia*

Origin: Central Asia, but species are indigenous to every continent.

Colors: Browns

Color Extraction: Please see the Walnut Hull Ink recipe on page 141.

Plant: Sun

Myths and Meanings: Intellect. Leonardo da Vinci and Rembrandt used walnut ink.

Healing Properties: Antioxidant, anti-inflammatory walnuts are rich in omega-3s. They support healthy digestion, balance blood sugar, lower blood pressure, and reduce the risk of obesity.

Magic: Protection, breakup. In the American Hoodoo tradition, walnut leaves and nuts are used to put jinxes on people. To fall out of love with someone, boil black walnuts in three quarts of water until the water reduces to one-third. Rub this water into your skin as you focus on your life without the person you wish to banish from your heart. Carry the water that's left and pour it out at a crossroads.

Other Traditional Uses: Used in the Bach flower essence recipe and furniture-making. Carved walnut shells are beloved toys and art forms in China. Walnuts are used in some cleaning products as an abrasive.

Part Three
REAP

Reaping immortal fruits of joy and love...
—JOHN MILTON

Now that you have cultivated your knowledge of plants and their power, it is time to reap what you have sown—transforming your magical practice. Each of these processes is both exciting and relaxing. They will fill your home with beautiful colors, scents, and powerful objects.

One of my students recently told me, "We live our lives online." This statement was imbued with grief and powerlessness. Through these projects and processes, you will reclaim your connection to the natural world—a place full of love, joy, and magic. By developing your Green Magic practice, you can transform how your life *feels*.

HARNESSING THE ELEMENTS TO EXTRACT PLANT COLOR

We extract color from plants to create artwork, practice artisanal traditions, and access magical botanical properties. The extraction processes relate to nature's elements: we reveal pigments by heating plants over the fire, soaking them in water, with freezing air, or pressing them against the earth. Whether you're extracting using your bubbling cauldron, a hammer, a freezer, or jars of water set in the sun, the color transformations of plants are evidence of the world's mysteries.

For a quick, easy experiment or to test how the color of a plant shifts when exposed to sunlight or oxygen, both the hapa zome and freezing processes work well. Plant cells, unlike animal cells, have cell walls. Freezing or smashing plants breaks these walls, releasing colorful pigments.

As you try out these processes, notice how they affect your body. Many of my students ferociously enjoy the release of emotion the hammering of a hapa zome brings. Smashing their hammers against the ground banishes the memories of a bad weekend, breaks the grip of anxiety, and makes you feel ridiculous, which is always good for you. Icy petals thawing tenderly under my warm fingertips when using the freezing process reminds me to be gentle—that all beings are delicate and deserve kindness. When I find powerful ink and use it to write or draw, I love watching it billow into pools of water, like strands of the incredible magic that connects us all. How does what you're doing and seeing make you feel? Note it in your grimoire.

Earth: Hapa Zome

Hapa zome means "leaf dye" in Japanese. This simple experiment incorporates the textures and shapes of plants into the design. Use this process to print on fabrics or paper—helpful in creating textile patterning, wrapping paper, greeting cards, natural artworks, or magic spells. It is immediately gratifying for those of all ages.

MATERIALS

- Watercolor or other heavy paper or light-colored fabric that has been washed and dried
- Plants
- A hammer

PROCESS

1) Gather your plants. Any plant may surprise you, so it is fun to experiment with those you see every day. If you are thinning or weeding your garden, this can be a good use for what you've removed.

2) If you're using paper, fold it in half and unfold it. Arrange the plants on one half of the fabric or paper.

3) After placing the plants, fold the other half of the fabric or paper on top of the plants and hammer on the material, thoroughly crushing the plants.

4) Open the folded fabric or paper. After the plants dry for a few minutes, wipe off the plant matter to see the patterns created.

5) Place the fabric or paper in indirect sunlight to dry.

Make notes in your grimoire about what colors the plants yielded and how their hues shifted over time.

Air: Freezing

Freezing plants breaks down their cell walls. So, as the plants thaw, they release their pigments upon contact. Frozen flowers are quick and easy to work with, making them fun for children.

MATERIALS

- Flowers and plants
- A freezer-safe container
- A freezer
- Your sketchbook or scrap paper
- Two sheets of watercolor or other heavy paper or light-colored fabric that has been washed and dried
- A heavy book

PROCESS

1) Collect your flowers and plants and place them in a freezer-safe container.

2) Put them in the freezer or outside in the cold, out of the sun.

3) Plan out your design in your sketchbook while waiting for the flowers to freeze—or set up your design spontaneously.

4) Once the flowers have frozen, remove them from the container. Working quickly, arrange them on one sheet of paper or fabric.

5) Place the second sheet of paper or fabric over the first.

6) Place the heavy book on top to press.

7) After fifteen minutes, carefully remove the book and the top sheet.

8) Allow both sheets to dry.

9) Gently remove the plant matter.

Water, Fire, and Air: Steam Eco-Printing

Eco-printing is a term that encompasses any process that transfers the shapes and colors of plants onto a surface. It typically indicates bundling plants into cloth and steaming them. For more on steaming bundles, please see Plant Bundles and Rose Curtains for the Winter Solstice on page 168.

Water and Fire: The Color Bath

Color baths create inks and dyes. Processing the baths produces dry pigments for paint-making. Color baths from natural materials are often less permanent than industrially developed colors. For *botanomancy* (which means plant magic), this impermanence is part of the magic. For art-making, we can photograph our work for digital reproduction or allow our projects to evolve.

Mordants and Binders

The first step in creating color baths is deciding what mordants you want on hand. In textile dyeing, the term *mordant* is used to describe a substance added to the color bath to affect the color or lightfastness of the pigment.

Some traditional mordants, like copper, tin, and chrome, harm both the environment and people. Luckily, we can use other substances from the kitchen to experiment with plant color creation.

Insoluble (More Permanent) Mordants include:

Alum	To brighten colors
Aluminum salts	To make dyes lightfast, washfast, and vibrant
Iron	To darken/sadden hues and produce blacks, browns, and grays. Create iron liquor by soaking iron objects in water for two weeks.
Soda ash	Used in tie-dyeing—very safe and increases the effectiveness of other mordants

Unfortunately, while relatively less toxic, these mordants are all mined. If you'd like to avoid materials produced by mining, try tannins as mordants.

Tannins are permanent and often employed to create natural fabric dyes. They include:

Acorns	**Oak galls**	**Walnut shells**
Black tea	**Pomegranate skins**	

We can also use soluble binders to create our baths. They are safer but won't last as long.

Other color shifters include:

Baking soda	**Salts**	**Vinegar**
Lemon juice	**Soy milk**	

Water and Baths

Now, we need to consider water. Water has chemical properties that affect color extraction. Like mordants, these additives can also shift the colors and affect the longevity of color baths. To avoid chemical interaction, use distilled water, untreated well water, or rainwater collected in a glass jar or stainless-steel container.

HARNESSING THE ELEMENTS TO EXTRACT PLANT COLOR

MATERIALS

Note: Specific materials needed for each process are listed with the recipes that follow. Like water, the materials you use to create color baths can affect the colors and properties of the baths. For example, a cast-iron cauldron will act as a mordant, shifting the properties of your baths. So it's considered a reactive material.

Nonreactive materials (materials that won't make your color bath react) are:

- Enamel
- Glass
- Marble
- Stainless steel
- Stone
- Wood

You can collect your materials at yard sales and secondhand stores.

Important: Keep your color experimentation materials separate from your cooking materials.

The Color Baths

There are several ways to create baths of beautiful plant color to be transformed into magic spells, inks, paints, stains, and dyes.

1. Traditional Color Bath

Making a color bath is usually achieved by simmering the plant material for thirty minutes to an hour, leaving the bath to cool overnight, and then straining the contents. Some plants only need to be soaked in hot water. Some can be dry, and others must be fresh. Each plant page in part two (page 39) notes the best recipe for extracting color. We can see how the colors change by experimenting with safe mordants (additives) from the kitchen—like salt, baking soda, alum, and lemon.

MATERIALS

Note: Please refer to the list of nonreactive materials on page 127. Be sure to keep your plant magic tools separate from your food preparation tools.

- Plant matter (leaves, sticks, blooms, and/or roots that you want to experiment with)
- Something to collect plants in (I use a basket, cloth bag, or a stainless-steel bowl.)
- A heat source in a well-ventilated location
- A nonreactive pot to simmer plants
- Water—enough distilled water or rainwater to cover the plant matter. Keep more water nearby to replenish the bath as needed.
- Measuring spoons in nonreactive materials
- Baking soda, salt, vinegar, alum, soda ash, lemon juice, or other kitchen chemicals to experiment with
- A nonreactive whisk, stick, or spoon to stir
- Paper strips for testing colors (Torn art papers work best.)
- Paintbrush for painting swatches in your grimoire
- Pencil for noting recipes
- A strainer and/or coffee filter

TO PRESERVE COLOR

- A glass jar
- A funnel
- A label or tape to use as a label
- A marker or pencil to write on the label
- Whole cloves, wintergreen oil, or thyme oil

PROCESS

1) **Gathering Plant Material**

   Gather the plant materials without crushing them.

2) **Storing the Plants for Ink-Making**

   You can use the plants immediately, or they can be frozen or dried. Heartier plants can be tied together and hung upside down with twine. I use a needle and thread to string the more delicate blooms together and hang them upside down to dry.

3) **Simmer the Plants**

   Cover the plant materials with water and simmer for one hour.

   As noted above, rainwater and distilled water are best.

4) **Strain the Liquid**

   Divide your solution into a few containers—one for each additive you want to try and one that you will keep additive-free. Pour the liquid through your strainer. If you'd like, you can add a coffee filter inside to catch small particles.

5) **Experiment with Chemicals from the Kitchen**

   Add a quarter teaspoon of salt, baking soda, soda ash, vinegar, or alum to each container. Label each container so you know which one you've used. Try other materials, too! As you experiment with adding more of each substance, use the quarter teaspoon to keep track of the amounts you've used.

   Place a small paper swatch in your container to check and see if the pigment is developing.

   When you have good color on your swatch, dip a watercolor brush into your solution and test the color.

Make sure to leave lots of color and moisture on the paper. Be sure not to tip your paper while your color is drying.

Make a note under each test swatch of what you used. Use a pencil so that the writing won't smudge.

NOTES

What is the date?

Which plant(s) did you use?

What water temperature did you use?

Dried or fresh flowers?

What chemical did you add? How much?

Notice that the color changes as the liquid dries. What happens if you wait an hour? What happens if you add more liquid?

Storing Your Color Bath

Choose a small jar for each of the colors you'd like to keep, and pour your baths into them using a funnel if needed. Add a clove or a few drops of wintergreen or thyme oil to prevent molding.

Label your jar with the plant, date, and ingredients. You can also write a note about where you collected it.

Use the colors immediately, or store them in a cool, dark place for later. When used for magic, the properties of the colors and flowers will imbue the inks with power.

2. Frozen Bath

MATERIALS

- Frozen plant matter
- A glass jar
- Water—rainwater or distilled water
- Sunlight
- Strainer
- A whole clove or a few drops of wintergreen or thyme oil to prevent molding

PROCESS

1) Place the frozen plant matter in a jar.
2) Cover the frozen plants with rainwater or distilled water, leaving half an inch of space at the top.
3) Seal the jar and set it in the sunshine. The colors will begin to leach out. Let the mixture soak overnight.
4) Squeeze and strain the plant material.
5) Add a whole clove or a few drops of wintergreen or thyme oil to prevent molding.

3. Sun Bath

MATERIALS

- Plant matter
- A glass jar
- Hot water
- Sunshine
- Strainer
- A whole clove or a few drops of wintergreen or thyme oil to prevent molding

PROCESS

1) Place the plant matter in a jar.
2) Cover the frozen plants with hot rainwater or distilled water, leaving half an inch of space at the top.
3) Seal the jar and set it in the sunshine. Let the mixture soak overnight.
4) Strain the plant material.
5) Add a whole clove or a few drops of wintergreen or thyme oil to prevent molding.

4. Processing Without Heat

Many plants can be ground to press the liquid out with a mortar and pestle.

Add water—a little at a time—as you crush the blooms to create a puddle of color.

Creating Dry Pigments

Lake pigments are dry pigments made from plants, often produced with the remnants of baths used to dye textiles. They can be less permanent and stable than commercially produced pigments. But the experience of brewing them is magical. They are also called *precipitated pigments*, because as the grains of color separate, they appear to rain down in the container.

Dry pigments can be stored for a long time and easily transported. Most paint-making recipes work with dry pigments.

MATERIALS

- A color bath in a large container with triple the space your bath takes up (For example, if your bath is one liter, you'll need a three-liter jar.)
- For each liter of your color bath, 10–30 grams of alum (for each quart, 2–6 tsp)
- For each liter of your color bath, 5–15 grams of soda ash (for each quart, 1–3 tsp)
- 2 small bowls of hot water
- Litmus paper to test pH
- Coffee filters and strainer

PROCESS

1) Place your color bath in the large container with three times more space than the bath takes up.

2) Dissolve ten grams (two teaspoons) of alum per liter (quart) of your color bath in a small amount of hot water.

3) Mix the alum solution into your color bath.

4) Dissolve the five grams (one teaspoon) of soda ash per liter (quart) of your color bath into the other small bowl of hot water.

5) Slowly add the soda ash solution to the color bath, stirring continuously as it bubbles. Be sure to go slow, or it will overflow! The mixture will be effervescent, releasing carbon dioxide.

6) The liquid should turn opaque as aluminum hydroxide forms, absorbs the pigments, and begins to rain down (precipitate).

7) Check the pH with the litmus paper to make sure it is neutral. Add pinches of acidic alum or alkaline soda to adjust as needed.

8) As the pigment settles, the top of the bath should be clear. If not, repeat the process to pull more stain from the bath.

9) Let the pigment settle for one day.

10) Strain the pigment using coffee filters. This process can take up to a day.

11) Allow the pigment to dry in the filter or the container of your choice. Jars, watercolor bowls, and acorn caps all work well.

Now you're ready to make paints and inks or add powdered pigments, imbued with the powers of color and properties of plants, to your magical creations.

Note: When working with any powdered substance, it is safest to use a filtration mask.

MAKING INKS AND PAINTS

I've taught paint-making for many years, but it wasn't until I began working on a National Institutes of Health grant project that I realized that natural art supplies could be a way around harmful chemical exposure. As part of the program, I taught teachers to make natural art supplies. One of the teachers replaced permanent markers with oak gall ink that she and her students brewed together, ridding her classroom of fumes and plastic. Soon, all their notes were painted with bamboo brushes. Everyone knew when something came from her class—all of their words looked magical.

Inks

Considered dangerous and subversive, most written records of ancient magic were destroyed. Discovering old secrets spun in spidery handwriting is a magic lover's dream. The inky documents we create, imbued with our loving intentions and the mystical properties of our homemade inks, will someday be treasured by those who find them.

Part pigment and part chemical reaction, inks go beyond just making marks. It is ink's nature to *engrave* parchment. Inks burn themselves into the surface they are applied to. While color baths can be used for multiple purposes, including dyeing and creating dry pigments, inks are created for immediate use. They flow easily enough to be used in pens and brushes and can be diluted into washes using water.

Natural ink recipes have been unchanged for thousands of years. These carefully brewed tones cover manuscripts from all over the ancient world. When we brew them today, we connect to ancestors all over the map of time.

You can use the process of creating a color bath as described on page 128 to create inks of varying stability and colorfastness. The process of turning magical plants into inks for spell-making is both relaxing and exciting. Soon, you'll have an apothecary of color, with each jar reminding you of a wonderful day hiking, cooking, or in the garden.

For the most stable, powerful, and permanent inks, you can turn to historic ink recipes—so ancient that no one knows who first created them.

Historic Ink Recipes

Use these inks for your powerful words.

Choose the colors that most resonate with your intentions.

Iron Liquor

Several ancient ink spells call for iron liquor, which can be used as an ink itself.

Before you embark on ancient ink-making, produce your own jar of iron liquor.

MATERIALS

- ¼–½ cup rusty objects (Some magic spells call for iron liquor made from 13 rusty nails.)
- A 32 oz glass jar
- 3 cups water, preferably distilled water or rainwater
- 1 cup white vinegar

PROCESS

1) Place the rusty objects in the jar and cover with the water and vinegar.

2) Leave the liquor to thicken uncovered, in a well-ventilated area away from children and animals for one to two weeks.

3) Stir before using. It will keep indefinitely and can be stored with its lid on once the iron has dissolved.

Acorn Cap Ink (Browns, Grays, Silvers)

For connection to the Otherworld

MATERIALS

- 1 cup acorn caps (see page 73)
- A nonreactive medium pot
- 2.5 cups distilled water or rainwater
- A burner to cook on
- A nonreactive spoon
- 5 drops iron liquor (see page 136)
- Paper scraps for testing color
- A strainer
- Coffee filters
- Glass jar
- Preservative (whole cloves, wintergreen or thyme essential oil)
- Label and marker

RECIPE

1) Rinse the acorn caps and put them in the pot.

2) Add 2.5 cups of distilled water or rainwater and five drops of iron liquor for every one cup of acorn caps.

3) Bring to a boil, cover pot, and lower to a simmer for two hours, adding more water as needed.

4) Check the color and liquid level. Continue to simmer to achieve the desired tone, adding more caps to go darker, more drops of iron liquor for more silver, or more water as needed.

5) Set aside portions of ink you like and continue experimenting with the rest, making notes in your grimoire.

6) When the ink is where you'd like it to be, pour it through a strainer and then filter it into a glass jar through a coffee filter.

7) Add the preservative to prevent molding.

8) Label the jar.

Buckthorn Berry Ink (Greens)

For love

Note: Buckthorn is healing for the skin but toxic to ingest. Please label this ink carefully and store it in childproof containers like old pill jars.

This recipe substitutes the traditional lye with safer and easier-on-the-ecosystem baking soda.

I've successfully created lovely, lasting green dye substituting telegraph weed (*Heterotheca grandiflora*), abundant in California, for buckthorn berries. I'm still testing this and haven't seen it in historical literature, but it's less poisonous and, for those of you in arid climates, it just might work! Also, try coffee berries for a similar green.

MATERIALS

- Gloves
- A medium-sized, dedicated pot
- 1 cup buckthorn berries
- A dedicated potato masher (or similar)
- Strainer
- Coffee filter
- 2 bowls
- ¼ tsp baking soda
- 1 tsp water
- Paper scraps for testing
- Glass container to store
- Preservative like whole cloves or essential oils of thyme or wintergreen

RECIPE

1) In a medium-sized dedicated pot, crush the berries with the masher.

2) Strain and filter into a bowl.

3) Separately, mix the baking soda with the water.

4) Add the baking soda solution, a couple of drops at a time, to the purple berry solution until it turns green.

5) Test the color using your paper scraps.

6) Store in a glass container with preservative—a whole clove or drops of the essential oils.

Oak Gall Ink (Purplish-Blacks)

For power and intuition

MATERIALS

- Oak galls ground to create ¼ cup oak gall powder (For more on oak galls see page 86.)
- A knife
- A spice or coffee grinder
- A nonreactive pot and spoon
- 2 cups distilled water or rainwater
- A burner to cook on
- Approximately 3 drops iron liquor (More may be necessary, depending on your galls.)
- Paper scraps for testing color
- Ashes (optional)
- Glass jars
- Labels and markers
- Preservative: whole cloves, wintergreen or thyme essential oil

RECIPE

1) Using the knife, crush or chop the oak galls.
2) Using a grinder, reduce them to a powder.
3) Place the powder in a pot. For every quarter cup of oak galls, add two cups of water.
4) Bring the mixture to a boil for five minutes.
5) Add drops of iron liquor to the cooling ink to shift the color from chestnut to purplish-black.
6) Pause when you have a color you like and set some aside.
7) Continue adding iron liquor to the mixture for deeper blacks, noting the amounts in your grimoire.
8) It is traditional to add ashes if the color is not deep enough, although I've not experienced this issue.
9) Put the inks into glass jars to store, labeling each one.
10) Add whole cloves or essential oils of thyme or wintergreen to the jars to prevent molding.

Pokeberry Ink (Red)

For passion

Note: Pokeberries are toxic. Store this ink in a childproof container (like an old pill bottle) labeled well. They grow wild throughout North America and can be gathered by the sides of trails, particularly in the Appalachians. If a safer red ink is needed, please consider substituting pomegranate (page 112) or cranberry (page 109). For more on pokeberry, see page 88.

MATERIALS

- Gloves
- A dedicated nonreactive potato masher or similar
- ½ cup pokeberries
- A dedicated, nonreactive pot or bowl
- A dedicated strainer
- Coffee filters
- Glass jar
- Label and marker
- Preservative: whole cloves, wintergreen or thyme essential oil

RECIPE

1) Wear gloves and, using utensils not used in your cooking, crush the berries in a nonreactive pot or bowl.

2) Strain the liquid.

3) Strain it once more, adding a coffee filter to the strainer.

4) Store in a clearly labeled container or use all the ink immediately. If you are storing, add a preservative to the jar to prevent molding.

Walnut Hull Ink (Sepia)

For grounding

MATERIALS

- Gloves (to avoid staining hands)
- 1 cup fresh walnut hulls
- A nonreactive pot
- Up to 5 cups distilled water or rainwater
- A burner to cook on
- Paper scraps for testing color
- A nonreactive slotted spoon
- A strainer
- An old T-shirt or coffee filter
- Glass jar
- Label and marker
- Preservative: whole cloves, wintergreen or thyme essential oil

RECIPE

1) Gather walnuts. If they are still green, keep them in the freezer for a week or so until they turn dark.

2) Place the walnut husks in the pot and cover them with water.

3) Bring to a boil, lower the heat, cover and then simmer for six to eight hours, adding more water as the level reduces.

4) Let the pot rest overnight.

5) Test the ink. Reduce the liquid by simmering uncovered to achieve darker colors.

6) Strain, pressing the moisture out of the husks. Filter through a T-shirt or coffee filter.

7) Store in a labeled glass jar and add the preservative to prevent molding.

Berry Ink (Kid-Friendly)

For fun

MATERIALS

- 1 cup frozen blueberries (Substitute frozen cherries, raspberries, or blackberries for more colors!)
- A potato masher
- A bowl
- A pot and burner (optional)
- A strainer (optional)
- A few cups (optional)
- Paper strips for color testing (optional)
- Water, baking soda, vinegar, or salt (optional)

RECIPE 1 (NO HEAT)

1) Smash berries.
2) Strain them.
3) Fingerpaint. Eat. Play. Yum!

RECIPE 2 (WITH HEAT)

1) Put the berries in a pot.
2) Cover them with water.
3) Simmer until they pop and their color fades.
4) Strain the liquid.
5) Test the color bath using paper strips. Make notes.
6) Separate the color bath into a few cups. Using the paper strips, test what happens to the color when you add baking soda, vinegar, or salt. Make notes.
7) Check what happens to the color when it dries. Make notes.

This is a great opportunity for sharing a science experiment with kids. You just did chemistry and created a completely unique ink!

Note: These inks change and fade quickly with time.

Paint-Making Recipes

Paint is created by adding concentrated color to a binder. The binder determines how thick the paint is and whether it is soluble in water or oil. To make paint, you need ground pigment or a reduced color bath. To create your own pigments, please see the precipitate bath recipe on page 133. After the pigment has dried, grind it until the grains are fine and even. Traditionally, this is done using a glass muller over a marble cutting board. Finely ground powder can also be achieved using a dedicated coffee grinder or spice mill.

To reduce a color bath made from any of the suggestions in part two, heat the bath and simmer until the water evaporates, leaving pigment of the desired intensity.

You can purchase ground natural pigments like beet powder, turmeric, and blue butterfly pea powder to get started with the primary colors.

Egg Tempera

Egg tempera is my favorite paint to make, especially with kids. Simple and stable, it has been used for thousands of years. It is thought to date back to ancient Egypt, and paintings created with its luminous layers have lasted centuries.

MATERIALS

- 1 egg
- Up to 1 tsp of the pigment of your choice
- 2 bowls
- A rubber spatula or palette knife (to stir)
- Up to 1 cup distilled water
- 2 jars (for leftovers, if any)

Please note that this recipe is not exact. It is traditional to add pigment slowly, keeping the paint loose and adding as little water as possible, or no water at all.

RECIPE

1) Carefully crack an egg over a bowl so the shell breaks in two halves and the egg yolk is sitting in one half. Some of the egg white will fall into the bowl.

2) Separate the yolk and egg whites by passing the egg yolk back and forth between the shells, letting the rest of the clear egg whites fall into the bowl.

3) Once the yolk is separated, set the bowl of egg whites aside.

4) Pour the egg yolk into your palm and set the eggshells aside.

5) Without breaking it, pass the egg yolk back and forth between your palms several times.

6) The outer membrane of the yolk will become dry.

7) Over the second bowl, carefully pluck the membrane from the yolk, letting the yolk's liquid center fall into the second bowl.

8) Discard the outer membrane.

9) Slowly stir your pigment into the yolk, a pinch at a time, thinning with distilled water if necessary until you have achieved the desired color saturation and consistency.

10) Use immediately. To paint with egg tempera, build your color with thin layers of paint.

11) The egg white is your glaze and can be brushed over the finished painting to add shine that makes the details pop. When not using it, you can store it in a jar in the fridge. If it dries out, you can loosen it with water.

12) You can store the paint in a glass jar in the refrigerator for a few days. Awaken dry paint with water. Save the eggshells to make gesso.

Watercolor

Watercolor is a simple, gorgeous, versatile, and sometimes difficult medium. Never thick, watercolor builds through layers of washes. There is no erasing in watercolor, so practitioners must embrace accidents. As old as the cave paintings, watercolor is pigment bound with gum arabic, which used to be made from the sap of two species of the acacia tree—a tree revered by ancient Egyptian and Hebrew peoples as a symbol of immortality. Gum arabic keeps the pigments connected and the undiluted paint creamy.

Watercolor Terminology

Watercolor paper comes in two forms: cold and hot press. Cold press paper is bumpy; hot press paper is smooth. Paper has weight—the higher the number, the thicker it is. To keep watercolor or mixed media paper from buckling, soak it or rinse it on both sides before painting, and press it to a flat surface.

Wet-on-wet technique is when watercolor washes are applied to wet paper, creating beautiful effects. Washes can be mixed beforehand by adding water to the pigment or created in the moment on the page. If you make a pool of water on an area of dry paper, the watercolor paint you apply will not leave the puddle. Wet-on-dry technique is when watercolor is applied to dry paper, giving the artist more control.

Sprinkling salt or gum arabic onto a still-wet, painted page produces exciting effects. Leftover wet watercolor paint can be allowed to dry in an open container. You can use a wet brush to awaken dry watercolor.

Fun containers for watercolor could include acorn tops, seashells, and bottle caps.

MATERIALS

- Teacup
- A teaspoon
- 1 tsp gum arabic powder
- 3 tsp boiling hot distilled water or rainwater
- 1 tsp honey—the runnier, the better
- 1 tsp pigment powder (You can purchase powders made from plants, or see lake pigments recipe on page 133.)
- Marble or granite grinding slab (or smooth cutting board able to withstand some pressure)
- Palette knife
- Glass muller (or similar)
- Watercolor containers

RECIPE

1) In the teacup, make a gum arabic solution by combining the gum arabic power with the boiling water. Stir until dissolved—this can take a while. Stir in the honey and set aside.

2) Add one teaspoon of pigment powder to the slab. Mixing with your palette knife, add up to one and a half teaspoons of gum arabic solution, pressing out any lumps.

3) Rub the glass muller in circles over the mixture until there is less friction and the muller's path is smooth and quiet.

4) Scrape the mixture into your watercolor containers with the palette knife. Allow to dry, and add water to awaken.

Gouache

If you love the look of comic books, southwestern pottery designs, or papyrus texts from ancient Egypt, then you are fond of gouache. For thousands of years, gouache has been used to create images formed from an aggregation of lines rather than washes. Gouache paintings tend to be delicate and controlled, detailed and linear. Adding chalk to the recipe makes the color more solid—and, sometimes, chalky.

MATERIALS

- A teacup
- A teaspoon
- 1 tsp gum arabic powder
- 5 tsp boiling hot distilled water or rainwater
- 1 tsp honey—the runnier, the better
- Pigment powder (You can purchase powders made from plants, or see lake pigments recipe on page 133.)
- Marble or granite grinding slab (or smooth cutting board able to withstand some pressure)
- 1 tsp ground chalk (optional)
- Palette knife
- Glass muller (or similar)

RECIPE

1) Make a gum arabic solution by combining the gum arabic powder with the boiling water in the teacup. Stir until dissolved—this can take a while. Stir in the honey and set aside.

2) Start by adding one teaspoon of pigment powder to the slab. To make more opaque paint, add one teaspoon of powdered chalk. Add a few drops of water. Mix out lumps with a palette knife.

3) Rub the glass muller in circles over the mixture until there is less friction and the muller's path is smooth and quiet.

4) Using the palette knife, scrape the mixture back into a blob. Add one teaspoon of the gum arabic solution. Mix well with a palette knife, adding another teaspoon of the solution if you'd like a looser, thinner paint.

5) After drying, your gouache painting will be stable and permanent. Leftover gouache can be stored in the refrigerator in a jar with a whole clove for a few months.

Encaustic

Encaustic is an ancient paint-making technique that incorporates beeswax as the binder to create a thick, luscious texture. Traditionally, encaustic paints are applied with a palette knife. The warm base hue of the beeswax makes the colors lovely.

The more modern recipes for encaustic involve petrochemicals, but here traditional oils are substituted. Olive oil is my favorite, but it's expensive. Any vegetable oil will do.

MATERIALS

- 1 cup beeswax
- A dedicated double boiler or Crock-Pot
- A burner to cook on
- A nonreactive spoon
- Up to ½ cup vegetable oil
- Up to ¼ cup pigment (You can use liquid pigment, purchase powders made from plants, or see lake pigments recipe on page 133.)
- 4 drops thyme or wintergreen essential oil
- A glass jar

RECIPE

1) Heat the beeswax on low heat in the double boiler or Crock-Pot until it softens (approximately 10 minutes).

2) Stir in the oil of your choice until the thickness is as desired. Please note that if you are using liquid pigment, you will want to keep the mixture slightly stiffer than desired at this stage.

3) Stir in the pigment, a little at a time, until the color is right.

4) Stir in the thyme or wintergreen oil.

5) Remove the encaustic paint from the heat, and spoon it into a jar. It will keep indefinitely, especially if kept refrigerated or cool. Let it warm to room temperature before use.

Family-Friendly Paint Recipes

Edible Finger Paint

This recipe is excellent for the young painter who puts everything in their mouth. The high chair tray makes an excellent surface for their creations and mixing palette.

MATERIALS

- 1 cup frozen mixed berries
- 1 small bowl for each kind of berry
- 1 cup vanilla or plain yogurt
- A high chair tray or wax paper fastened to a table

RECIPE

1) Sort the mixed berries into different bowls, allowing them to thaw.

2) Squash out their juices, and remove the berries (great for making baby food).

3) Add dollops of yogurt and mix with each juice.

4) Use the bowls to create delicious paintings!

Milk Paint

This remarkably stable paint recipe comes from the medieval period.

MATERIALS

- 1 cup milk, or for thicker paint, condensed milk
- 4 small bowls
- 1 tbsp each of fruit and vegetable juices for edible paints (Or use traditional pigment to create permanent paints. The paint will be stable when dry, but berry pigments are impermanent. For longer-lasting paint, use some of the more permanent color materials in part two of this book, like nettle.)
- Spoons
- Paintbrush
- Watercolor or mixed media paper
- Glass storage containers
- Labels and markers

RECIPE

1) Separate the milk into four small bowls of a quarter cup each.

2) Add juices to each milk until the color is right.

3) Try out your paints on watercolor or mixed media paper!

4) Unused paint does not store well. You can try keeping it in a labeled glass jar in the refrigerator overnight.

Puffy Paint

MATERIALS

- ¼ cup salt
- ½ cup white flour
- Mixing bowl
- Spoon
- ½ cup water
- 1 tbsp sand
- Containers or squeeze bottles
- 2 tbsp powdered pigments or color baths (or more, if needed)

RECIPE

1) Combine the salt and flour in the bowl and stir.

2) Add the water and sand.

3) Separate the mixture into different containers or squeeze bottles.

4) Add color baths or pigments and mix well.

5) Squeeze or apply paint to make a puffy painting. Paper and other porous surfaces work best.

6) Allow to dry for twenty-four hours.

Note: Unused paint will keep for a week in the refrigerator but must be brought to room temperature to use again.

Using Paints and Inks to Inspire, Calm, and Access Your Magic and Otherworld Senses

This series of meditative spells will ground and connect you, while helping you attain creative joy. These exercises can result in perfectly imperfect, beautiful magical pools of color. Embrace the mess, and honor the process, losing control and letting the energy of the universe guide your hand.

Painting Spells: Interconnection

Sky-to-Sea Spell

A spell to encourage creativity and connect you to the water worlds—above and below

Of all the elements, water is most associated with creativity. Water from the sky wakes the seeds in spring. We grow into life in the waters of our mother's womb. Our bodies wither without water.

The sky is filled with water—great soaring rivers of water vapor in banks made of wind.

The water cycle draws from the earth. Evaporations from tiny, scattered dewdrops or vast warm seas rise and combine to create our fluid atmosphere.

The sky reciprocates, giving us back life-giving rains and snows. We all drink it in—the soils, the plants, the animals, the people. Everything is connected.

No one is alone.

Create a painted sea-to-sky spell to reconnect with the water and nourish your creativity.

MATERIALS

- Soaked watercolor or mixed media paper (Any size that feels comfortable will work—larger is often easier.)
- A flat surface to lay the paper on (a canvas, cardboard, back of a cookie sheet, etc.)
- A small jar of water-soluble blue paint (tempera, watercolor) or ink
- A larger brush, round or flat
- A jar of water
- A towel
- Small jars of red or yellow paint (optional)

PROCESS

1) Place the soaking-wet paper on the flat surface.

2) Gaze up at the sky. Notice that the higher you look, the deeper the sky's blue or the darker its gray. This is because of the movement of the atmosphere and how water vapor gathers close to the land. Breathe in and whisper:

> *Many waters,*
> *Wandering waters,*
> *The waters in me*
> *wandered through the sky.*
> *The waters in me*
> *rose from the sea.*

3) Plunge your brush into the blue paint or ink, picking up a lot of color.

4) Sweep your brush along the top edge of your paper, creating a dark blue line. Paint another line just below and slightly overlapping the first. Repeat without adding more paint so that the lines get lighter as you move lower, creating a fading or ombré effect. Continue until you reach two-thirds of the way down the page. This is the sky.

5) Plunge your brush back into the blue paint or ink.

6) Sweep your brush along the bottom edge of your paper, creating another dark line of blue. Paint another line just above and slightly overlapping the first. Repeat, moving upward until you meet the pale line of your sky.

7) On your page, sea meets sky. Rinse your brush and dry it using the towel. Once completely dry, your brush will lift color from the page. Experiment with using it to lift cloud shapes from the sky. Mirror them in the sea below.

8) You can also experiment with making mountain shapes (they will be darkest at the top) or adding other colors to create fields or sunshine, knowing you don't have control over the watery painting. You can just enjoy the beautiful surprises you create.

Ink Divination

A spell to find answers

Have you ever looked at a tree, a cloud, or a mountainside and seen a face looking back at you? Perhaps it is because someone from the Otherworld wants to communicate with you. Use this same noticing with your inks.

MATERIALS

- A small jar of ink
- Paper (1 half sheet for each question)
- A brush
- A small jar of water

PROCESS

1) If possible, select an ink of a color and materials related to your question. For example, to ask about love, use pokeberry ink. To connect your question to the Otherworld, use a purplish oak gall ink. (You can find color meanings on page 163 and plant meanings in part two. Or choose an ink that calls to you for mysterious reasons.)

2) Place your paper in front of you horizontally.

3) Close your eyes. Breathe deeply and ask a question.

4) Plunge your brush into the jar of water and hold it over your paper, letting the water drip from it to create puddles and patterns of droplets.

5) When you feel ready, place your brush in the ink and lightly touch the pooling water. Let the color surge into the water.

6) As you add color, it will create images that look like clouds moving across the sky. Read these images as though they are a visual message just for you that changes as you concentrate, asking more questions.

7) Continue interacting with the ink on the page. The face or symbol of who you are communicating with will emerge in the ink.

Ink divination for a yes or no answer

To answer a yes-no question, write "Yes" and "No" opposite each other on a paper. In between, paint a pool of clear moon water. (Moon water is water left outside in a clear container all night under the full moon.) Now, speak your question aloud and add a single drop of ink into the pool's center. Whatever word it drifts toward is the answer to your question.

Layered Letters

An ancient manifesting spell

MATERIALS

- 1 small jar of ink or paint
- Paper
- A brush or pen
- A candle
- A pinch of salt

PROCESS

1) When possible, choose inks and paper of the color and materials that suit your intention. For example, use red rose petal wash to inquire about love and awaken sexuality or lavender water to calm and connect your emotions to the Otherworld.

2) Write or paint an intention on a piece of paper.
   Example: *I will find true love.*

3) Cross out all the vowels.
   Example: We are left with *w l l f n d t r l v*

4) Cross out all the repeated consonants.
   Example: Now we have *w l f n d t r v*

5) Write or paint these remaining letters connected into an interlocking design or layered over each other.

6) To close, light a candle and sprinkle salt into it, whispering your thanks to your ancestors.

7) Keep the paper in your pocket or a special place in your home.

COLOR MAGIC

When I was a child, I would tire early of winter. In February, I'd start to check for the small purple flowers called crocuses every morning, trudging out to a particular spot where two leafless maple trees interlaced their creaking branches overhead, scanning the unbroken snow. Crocuses were always the first plants to emerge. Eventually, the snow would soften and shrink. I'll never forget the sight of the first sharp-tipped green leaves poking through the last layer of melting snow. I remember running to tell my sisters crocuses were coming.

The first crocuses are miracles of spring! Small, soft, and so lusciously purple. Just as the crocuses bloomed, the forsythia would explode into a festival of yellow blossoms. Yellow daffodils weren't far behind. I grew to associate purple and yellow with spring's beginnings.

Summer was a riot of color, ending in the time of blue blooms—cornflowers, delphiniums, sea holly, salvia—that continued to dazzle as autumn's orange palette of marigolds, chrysanthemums, squash, and turning leaves began to overtake the landscape.

By midwinter, the palette became red and green. Holly berries and conifer hues sang out the loudest through the snow.

At the age of sixteen, I received a scholarship to art school. I left the forest and made my way to New York City, where I enrolled in a class called Color Theory. We spent five hours each week sliding squares of silk-screened papers across a white artboard to learn how colors interact with each other. And then, late at night, we spent a few more hours carefully cutting the papers and rubber cementing them in formations that demonstrated our discoveries about how color behaves.

My teacher was a student of Josef Albers, who wrote the book *The Interaction of Color*. In doing so, Albers started a new field of study based on the ideas of a poet named Johann Wolfgang von Goethe.

In 1810, Goethe published the first color wheel.

He made his wheel to illustrate his theory that colors change in relation to each other. They look different in different contexts. Colors affect each other, and the way they shift affects our emotions.

Based on Goethe's wheel, we learned that every color has an opposite that complements it perfectly. Complementary colors sit across from each other on the color wheel. In each pair, one is a primary color—a color that cannot be created by mixing two colors—and one is a secondary color—a color created by combining two primary colors.

THE COMPLEMENTARY COLORS

Primary Color + Secondary Color

Yellow + Purple (mix of Blue and Red)

Blue + Orange (mix of Yellow and Red)

Red + Green (mix of Yellow and Blue)

I was astonished! These were the color pairings to which I had mapped my understanding of the seasons.

I raised my hand to ask my teacher about the first colors of spring. I didn't phrase the question well, and nobody understood what I was asking. So, embarrassed, I kept my wonderings to myself.

Over the next twenty years, as I made my way across the country, I kept noticing complementary colors sharing space together in nature. I kept quietly wondering.

And then, I read a passage in *Braiding Sweetgrass* by botanist Dr. Robin Wall Kimmerer. She discusses the phenomenon she had noted as a student—how purple asters bloom near the yellow goldenrod. She wondered why they complemented each other so beautifully. She says:

> *Growing together, both [the asters and the goldenrod] receive more pollinator visits than they would if they were growing alone. It's a testable hypothesis; it's a question of science, a question of art, and a question of beauty.*

Pollinators find complementary colors irresistible, too? I was so excited when I read this. Nature speaks lovingly and joyfully to us all through color!

Art Wound

My Color Theory teacher didn't mean to make me feel silly. And neither do the many art teachers who accidentally make their young students feel like they are "not good at art" or "are doing it wrong." But so many of the children and adults I work with struggle with what I call "the Art Wound."

How painful it is to feel shame when we open our hearts to create. How isolating to think that we can't speak nature's language properly.

To be creative is to be very brave, to do something risky. To be creative makes us feel vulnerable. Choosing to be creative is constructive, connecting you to nature's magic. There is no "right way" to draw something. There is a way that only *you* draw something. The uniqueness of your art is one of the special gifts you bring to your relationship with creation.

Healing the Art Wound through Color

I recommend starting by doing something you have absolutely no control over. Paint on soaking wet paper with tempera paint! There is no possible way that you can manage the outcome of water-soluble paint on soaking-wet paper—and that's why you should try it.

To start, you could create a color wheel.

Color Wheel Healing Spell

MATERIALS

- **1 large sheet of mixed media or watercolor paper that has been soaked in water** (I soak mine in a cookie sheet in a pinch.)
- **A board, cardboard, canvas, or the back of a cookie sheet** to lay the wet paper on
- **A pencil**
- **Small jars of red, yellow, and blue paint**, preferably tempera (Acrylic and watercolor work well, too, but acrylic will not wash out of clothes, and watercolor can be a bit less brilliant.)
- **A bigger brush** (I prefer a size 19 round brush, but use what you can.)
- **A larger jar of water** to clean your brush

PROCESS

1) Pick up your paper and let some water drip from one corner.
2) Lay the wet paper on your canvas, board, or back of your cookie sheet.
3) Draw a circle in pencil on the paper and divide it into three pie pieces. It will look like a peace sign.
4) Start with the lightest color. Dip your brush into the yellow paint and paint the first pie piece yellow.

The color will run. It will not stay in the lines.

Let it. No matter what you do, you can't control the color.

Enjoy the vibrant, beautiful color of yellow, connected to your inner fire and intuition, located in the chakra of your solar plexus.

As you move the yellow paint over the watery triangle, breathe into your solar plexus.

As you work with yellow, feel your fire flare.

5) Submerge your brush into the jar and tap it on the bottom until it's clean.

6) Dip your brush into the red paint. Paint the next piece of the pie red, again letting the color flow. Allow the edges of the red and yellow to mix and begin to create orange, the color of nurturing.

Imagine the powerful color of red coursing through you as you paint. Red is connected to your creativity and passion and the chakra at your spine's base.

As you work with red, feel your creativity surge.

7) After cleaning your brush again, check to make sure your paper is still wet. If it isn't, sprinkle some water on it.

8) Now, plunge your brush into the blue, pulling lots of color from deep in the jar. Take a deep breath and paint your last pie piece blue, letting green (love and interconnectedness) and purple (spiritual connection) begin to form on either side as it mixes with yellow and red.

Blue is the color of communication. As you work with blue, breathe and feel your throat opening. You sense anything that has been blocking you loosen.

As you work with blue, you can speak your truth.

9) There should be a messy pool of beautiful colors in front of you. What is it telling you? You may want to add more of a primary color, more water, or encourage more intermingling.

Perhaps it says, "Stop now and take a picture of this."

Let the colors speak to you.

10) When you reach your stopping place, leave your painting on the painting board. Set your painting board somewhere warm and flat to dry.

*As you repeat this experience, delighting in the colors,
staying in the moment, and not using the word should,
you will
free yourself from perfectionism,
open to your unique creative power,
and heal.*

Color, Emotions, and Energy

The language of color can be simultaneously universal and deeply personal. Across centuries and cultures, colors have had specific meanings for our bodies, minds, and spirits. Culture, environment, and our physiology affect how and how many colors we perceive.

Learning to pay attention to our emotional responses to colors can tell us what colors mean to us.

Close your eyes and imagine each primary and secondary color in turn.

Red. Orange. Yellow. Green. Blue. Indigo. Violet.

What feelings, memories, or words come to mind? What do these colors mean to you? Create a personal color key by noting your response to each one.

Once we understand the meaning of colors, we can invite their energy to support us as we move through the day. We can spend time with, forage for, eat, plant, and collect items that help us invite this color energy into our lives.

*Thank you, Mother Nature, for the language of color.
Thank you for speaking with me.*

Color Magic Cards

Now that you know more about your relationship to the colors and their meanings, you can make Color Magic Cards to answer questions, help clarify your hopes, and calmly make choices.

Having a set of homemade Color Magic Cards imbued with the full array and powers of plant pigments can help you focus your senses and intentions.

MATERIALS

- 1 large sheet of watercolor paper of your choice
- A paintbrush
- A jar of water in which to wash the brush
- 7 colors of paint—every primary and secondary color plus black
- A flat surface that can be stained, like a canvas, cardboard box, or the back of a cookie sheet

PROCESS

1) Fold the paper in half three times, until it is divided into eight rectangles.
2) Unfold and refold the paper, bending the creases backward to recreate the eight rectangles.
3) Repeat until the creases are loose and fraying.
4) Tear the paper in half along the first fold. Continue tearing in half along the folds until you have eight cards.
5) Set one card aside. This will be your white card.
6) Paint each remaining card with clean water on both sides.
7) Press them to your flat surface.
8) Paint each wet card a different color.
9) Allow them to dry.

After they have dried, you may use these cards in various ways:

- Spread them out to find which colors are calling you today.

- Shuffle the cards with your eyes closed, and then pick one. Which color did you select? What is it telling you?

- Pick two cards. One means *yes*, and one means *no*. Trust your senses to discern which is which. Turn them over and shuffle them as you ask your question. Pick one to see the answer.

- Invite a friend to pull the card they are most drawn to. Ask them about what that color means to them.

- Choose a color to use in a spell or meditation. The card will help you focus on the color and fix your intentions.

- Sleep with a card under your pillow to influence your dreams.

- Bring them with you to remind you that color is nature's way of telling you that you are beautiful.

Color Cards for Spell Work: Create a color card dyed, painted, or printed with a plant color that will strengthen your spell. For written spells, plant the card in the earth to manifest something. Burn the card to banish.

Color Meanings

You may find that your reaction to a particular color is the same as other people's. Certain colors have been associated with certain ideas, emotions, and philosophies for thousands of years. Selecting plant colors—be it their blooms or working with colors you've extracted by writing, painting, staining, or anointing with them—adds power to your spells and rituals. Colors and the tones black and white have traditional meanings in magic:

- Brown: Home and hearth, finding lost things
- Pink: Nurturing and emotional healing
- Red: Passion, courage, and survival instincts
- Orange: Creativity, passion, sensuality, pleasure
- Yellow: Inspiration, your soul's purpose
- Green: Abundance, attraction, interconnectedness, love
- Blue: Speaking truth, listening, and forgiveness
- Indigo: Divination, meditation, connecting psychic abilities
- Purple: Wisdom from the Otherworld
- Gold: The sun, health, energy, good luck
- Silver: The moon, dreams, abundance
- Copper: Money, success, career growth
- Black: Protection, banishing threats, grounding, safety
- White: Peace, balancing energy

Breathe the Colors: An Air Spell

To reset, focus on or imagine flowers of specific colors and imagine you are breathing them into the corresponding places in your body indicated below:

RED • Breathe red into the base of your spine to support your instincts, promote feelings of belonging, and remember your earliest memories.

    Relating to the element: Earth
    From Vedic tradition: *Muladhara* (root chakra)

ORANGE • Breathe orange into your pelvis to support your sexuality, creativity, and fertility.
    Relating to the element: Water
    From Vedic tradition: *Svadhisthana* (sacral or pelvic chakra)

YELLOW • Breathe the yellow into your navel to connect your soul's energy to your purpose. Trust your intuition.
    Relating to the element: Fire
    From Vedic tradition: *Manipura* (navel chakra)

GREEN • Breathe green into your heart to enhance your feeling of interconnectedness, compassion, and love.
    Relating to the element: Air
    From Vedic tradition: *Anahata* (heart chakra)

BLUE • Breathe blue into your throat to speak your truth and listen deeply. Connected to the *ether* aspect of the fifth element (the clear sky, the atmosphere's upper regions, beyond the clouds).
    From Vedic tradition: *Vishuddha* (throat chakra)

INDIGO • Breathe indigo into your forehead to support your insight and groundedness.
    It is connected to the *divine light* aspect of the fifth element (the light of creation).
    From Vedic tradition: *Ajna* (third-eye chakra)

PURPLE • Breathe purple into the top of your head to connect to the spiritual realm and understand who you are beyond your physical self.
    It is connected to the *unified* fifth element—cosmic energy.
    From Vedic tradition: *Sahasrara* (crown chakra)

SEASONAL CALENDAR OF NATURAL ARTS PROJECTS

Whenever you give a blessing, a blessing returns to enfold you.
—JOHN O'DONOHUE

The Mystery of Plants

Creating plant magic is a mysterious process. Sometimes, we don't know which plants will provide intense sensations or colors. We can experiment with all parts of the plant. A tree's outer bark may make the most potent spells. The inner bark may offer deep pigments. Simple leaves may make gorgeous, detailed hapa zome prints. Wild berries may shift to unexpected hues when combined with natural additives from the kitchen.

Explore all this with the intention of experimentation and forming new relationships with the landscape.

We don't know how the visual spells, inks, or color baths we create will shift over time. Using digital photography, we can preserve and share the temporary. Keeping records of ephemeral textures and tones means you can incorporate them into collages and illustrations later.

Altered Books for Autumn

In many magical traditions, autumn is the beginning of the magical year. In autumn, we reap the harvest. We say goodbye to long days and embrace change as a part of life. We come close to the Otherworld as the veil thins. We have an opportunity to work with our shadow sides.

As we traverse this period, we may want to collect colorful leaves or do rubbings from ancestral gravestones. We might create little colorful painted

spells. We may feel called to journal and explore the parts of ourselves that we keep hidden. Creating a scrapbook journal for the year will manifest a place where you can collect your treasures and words.

Using an altered book technique—where you find an old book and transform it by coloring, writing, and collaging over its pages—can be exciting and liberating. The printed page offers excellent visual opportunities—the textures of the words, the effect of removing or highlighting them, and the interaction with existing illustrations. It is freeing to work on a page that isn't blank in a book that isn't pristine.

MATERIALS

- An old book, perhaps one that the library has put out to give away
- 1 bottle of glue
- Natural materials—amount is optional
- ½ cup white paint or gesso (If you are using gesso, you may want to use a fine grit sandpaper to soften the pages.)
- Pens and paints
- Ribbon or twine

PROCESS

1) Find a book that you'd like to work with. It can be one that you have extra copies of, an obsolete instruction book, or a catalog.

2) Using art and natural materials and collage, alter the book with your own content. You can use white paint or light washes to mute the page contents, leaving some unaltered words.

3) When not using the book, leave it slightly open in a sunny spot or near a heat source to dry. If the book begins to get puffy and expand, remove unused pages and press the book under several heavy books.

4) Tie the book shut with a ribbon or twine.

Plant Bundles and Rose Curtains for the Winter Solstice

When it's time to brace against the cold, having colorful curtains can help. Print cheering, cozy window dressings with collected dried plants, fresh herbs in your garden, or flowers you purchased in a winter bouquet. Their colors and shapes will brighten up your room and remind you of the spring to come.

With dried plant materials, experimenting with steam will give you the opportunity to use a warm process that humidifies the winter's air. With fresh plants, you can use a hapa zome technique that releases the plants' scents into the air.

For a smaller-scale project, you can print on bandanas, linen napkins, or socks.

MATERIALS FOR WORKING WITH DRIED PLANTS

- White or light-colored cotton curtains or other cloth objects
- Dried plants—enough to create a pattern over the entire cloth
- A roll of parchment paper
- A dowel or bamboo pole the cloth can roll onto, meaning it is slightly wider than the cloth.
- 12 inches of string or twine
- A steamer pot that can accommodate the cloth roll and pole

MATERIALS FOR WORKING WITH FRESH PLANTS

- White or light-colored curtains or smaller cloth objects
- Fresh flowers, leaves, and stems
- A hammer

PROCESS

Fresh Plants

Please follow the hapa zome process on page 123.

Dried Plants

1) For curtains, skip this step. For all other cotton objects, launder the cotton and brush it with soy milk. Dry.
2) Lay out the cloth and arrange the dried plant materials. Select your dried plants with intention and limit your palette to reflect your wishes for the best designs.
3) Lay a parchment paper over the design.
4) Place the dowel, pole, or stick at one end and roll the fabric tightly around it.
5) Tie the bundle together.
6) Place the bundle in the steamer and steam gently for one to two hours, peeling back a corner to check the printing.
7) When you're satisfied with the color, remove the bundle. Snip the strings and hang the fabric on the pole out to dry.

Natural Egg Dyes for Spring

Not just for or Oestre, or Easter, eggs are a symbol across cultures of fertility or the renewal of life. Create natural dyes with beets, onion skins, turmeric, and blueberries. Print on the eggs with wildflowers for an astonishingly beautiful, healthy-to-eat family tradition. If you blow out the eggs' centers, you can keep them as a decoration for many years. You can use this process with your leftover dyes to decorate cloth, paper, or yarn.

MATERIALS

- Spring flowers and leaves—two for each egg

- White or bright-colored eggs (Keep the egg carton!)

- Thumbtack and bowl (optional—to blow out egg centers)

- 2 cups each of nontoxic edible dye matter in a variety of colors (e.g., blueberries, turmeric, onion skin, and beets)

- Pots for each of the dye materials

- Approximately 1–2 cups water per color (Tap water works well.)

- Vinegar (optional)

- Spoon

- White scraps of paper (for testing colors)

- Cups for soaking eggs in each color

- Cheesecloth or another porous cloth that can be wrapped tightly around an egg (Old nylon stockings work well!)

PROCESS

1) Gather edible flowers and leaves. (See part two for examples.) These flowers will be used to create patterns on the eggs. Some of the flowers and leaves will transfer their pigments as well.

2) Either cook or blow out the centers of the eggs. The best way to cook the eggs is to steam them for about eleven minutes and then place them in an ice bath. This is because when it's time to eat them, the shells of steamed eggs are easier to remove than those of boiled eggs. The ice bath will help the cooked eggs stay perfectly rounded.

    Uncooked eggshells that have their centers blown out will never go bad. To accomplish this, use a thumbtack to poke and carve a hole at each end of the egg. Bring the egg to your lips and blow really, really hard on the hole at one end as you hold the egg over a bowl. Eventually, the yolk and white will emerge from the other end, the interior will dry, and the egg can be kept indefinitely. Use the bowl of yolks and whites to create a spring custard or quiche.

3) Select the dye materials and prepare the pots. To make simple, natural egg dyes that can be mixed to create all the colors, we use:

    - Blueberries for blue
    - Turmeric for yellow
    - Beets for red

Onion skins are also a lovely option. Any shade of onion skin gives a beautiful color when boiled.

For more on using blue, yellow, and red to mix other colors, please see page 156.

Place the ingredients in separate pots. Cover them with water or a mixture of one part water to two parts vinegar. (Vinegar may make the colors more vivid.)

4) Bring each pot to a boil and lower the heat, simmering uncovered for up to thirty minutes.

5) Use your spoon to press more pigment from the plant materials.

6) Test dyes by submerging scraps of white paper in the baths for a few minutes. Remove the strips and let them dry to see how the color shifts when exposed to oxygen. The papers' torn edges will reveal a more saturated color that resembles what the eggs could look like after a longer soak.

If your color is too light, add more berries, herbs, beets, or skins and stir. Bring the pot back to a simmer with the lid off and test the color again in twenty minutes.

7) When the baths are colorful enough, pour some of each bath into three or more different cups. Use your primary colors to mix new colors. Play with the colors until you have the palette of dyes you desire.

8) Shake off any bugs and wrap the wildflowers and leaves you've collected over the eggs. Wrap the covered eggs tightly in cheesecloth, an old nylon stocking, or similar material so that the plant matter is pressed tight against the eggshells.

9) Submerge the eggs into the dye pots or cups of mixed dyes and leave them soaking for at least ten minutes. Longer soaks will produce deeper colors.

10) When you are satisfied with the color, place the eggs lightly back into their carton to dry. You will see their colors change as they are exposed to the air.

11) After the eggs are dry, carefully cut the cloth and remove it.

12) Gently peel away the flowers and leaves. Rub to remove any plant residue.

Bath Salts for Summer Solstice

Making bath salts is simple and affordable. Salt crystals are full of healing and renewing energy. But it's possible the best bath salts aren't salts at all. Available in any drugstore, Epsom salts are sold in bulk. Because they are crystallized magnesium, they promote relaxation, calming the central nervous system. A bath infused with Epsom salts will dramatically ease muscle pain.

An Epsom salt bath will make you feel warm, as though the water is hotter than it is. It will also make you thirsty, so it's important to have plenty of water nearby before you step into the bath. Make these bath salts as blessing gifts for loved ones at the height of summer to help them in the cold months to come or as a relaxing gift.

MATERIALS

- A bowl (steel, copper, ceramic, or wood)
- 3 cups Epsom salts
- A clear bottle or jar with a lid
- A wood, steel, or silver spoon
- A funnel and a chopstick (optional)
- A label or gift tag
- ½ cup baking soda (optional) (This will help keep your salts fragrant. Note that its gases can build up in a sealed jar at high altitudes, causing it to break.)

VARIATIONS

(Choose which works for your bath)

Experiment with combinations. For example, lavender combines well with almost everything. It is particularly effective with orange and eucalyptus. You can also add a quarter teaspoon of vanilla extract to a cinnamon bath. Rose or lemon softens a basil bath and adds positive intention.

FOR RELAXATION: Lavender flowers, leaves, and/or 20 drops of essential oil

FOR SPIRITUAL CLEANSING AND WOUND TREATMENT: 1½ cups pink sea salt

FOR LOVE: Rose petals and/or 20 drops of essential oil

FOR DECONGESTION: Eucalyptus leaves and/or 20 drops of essential oil

FOR FOCUS AND EMOTIONAL BALANCE: Clary sage leaves or 20 drops of essential oil

FOR SKIN CARE: Apple cider vinegar and an additional ½ cup baking soda

FOR WARMTH: Cinnamon

FOR CHEERFULNESS: Dried citrus peels or 20 drops of sweet orange essential oil

FOR PROTECTION: Dried basil

FOR MAGIC: Add dried mugwort to any of the above.

PROCESS

1) In the bowl, mix the Epsom salts with the additive(s) of your choice. If you choose to add baking soda, stir it in as well.

2) Spoon the salt mixture into the glass container. If the container has a narrow top, you can use a funnel and a chopstick to push material into the bottle.

3) Create a label complete with a special blessing and instructions to use a half cup per bath while drinking lots of water.

CREATING YOUR OWN GRIMOIRE

This book is full of Green Magic secrets and experiments connecting nature's magic, history, mythology, biology, cuisine, and craft. With each exploration, you deepen your perceptions of the seen and unseen. You scry the world and how it moves through the seasons in new ways. You sense the interplay of the elements, within and without. With this new vision, you can harness the powers of plants with all your senses.

You can fill your own grimoire—your book of magic—with your observations of the world's mystery, how you move through it, and how it moves through you. With this knowledge, experience, and discernment comes the power to create magic spells.

Constructing Spells with the Elements

Plants are magic. In Shakespeare's *Macbeth*, three witches stir a cauldron and chant the recipe for a spell. The ingredients sound gory, but the recipe is actually a list of plants using their British folk names:

Eye of newt, and toe of frog,
Wool of bat, and tongue of dog,
Adder's fork, and blind-worm's sting,
Lizard's leg, and howlet's wing,
For a charm of powerful trouble,
Like a hell-broth boil and bubble.

Eye of newt	Mustard seed
Toe of frog	Buttercup
Wool of bat	Moss
Tongue of dog	Houndstongue
Adder's fork	Violet
Blind-worm's sting	Knotweed
Lizard's leg	Ivy
Howlet's wing	Garlic

Witches design their spells based on the properties of the plants, their colors, and their relationship to the elements. For thousands of years, people worldwide have employed plants for spiritual and healing practices, using them for magic. All of life, when it dies, eventually nourishes tiny green shoots. There is profound power in this transformation.

Throughout this chapter, various spells will call for plants or herbs relating to the desired outcome. To select your plants, refer back to the grimoires of part two, which detail the properties, powers, and possibilities of petals, leaves, and roots.

Intentions

The most powerful magic happens when you set an intention and pay attention to it each day, giving it the energy and effort it needs to manifest. Spells help us name our intentions and focus on them. You can design your own spells using the plants discussed in this book.

As you choose the components you wish to use in your spells, consider the following:

The Elements: Design your spell as a small ritual incorporating the elements you feel will help you.

The Process: Incorporate your favorite magic: writing, speaking, breathing, singing, moving, lighting candles, drawing, cooking, gardening, etc.—all of this is magic.

The Ingredients: Collect the ingredients to create your spell. These don't necessarily need to be physical ingredients. They can also be sounds, light, thoughts, and smells.

As you collect, think about the preceding example spells and incorporate the following considerations.

Applying the Elements to Spell and Ritual Design

The elements can be incorporated into your spell design as a place to cast your spell or a force that transforms your ingredients as they transform you—i.e., you can burn them, wet them, blow on them, or bury them. Combining elements in a specific order creates a special power.

Add fire to earth: scorching, healing, and rebirth
Add earth to fire: calming, an end

Add fire to water: danger and secrets
Add water to fire: extinguished danger, no secrets

Add water to earth: sharpness, reshaping form
Add earth to water: softness

Add earth to air: suffocation
Add air to earth: the cycle of abundant life

Add air to fire: life, vibrancy
Add fire to air: consumption, exhaustion

Add air to water: movement and gravity
Add water to air: stillness and impermanence

Plant Meaning

Part two of this book lists the historical meanings or energies of the featured plants. Incorporate these meanings as you design your spell.

For quick reference, here is a list, but please refer to the earlier grimoires for a more in-depth meaning:

For Balance	Cinnamon, mint, prickly pear/nopal, sagebrush, turmeric, walnut
For Clarity	Fennel, mint, spinach, star anise
For Courage	Black tea, chili, chives, nettle, purple basil, rosemary
For Fertility	Avocado, carrots, chili pepper, cinnamon, citrus, mint, spinach
For Happiness	Black tea, borage, cherry, cinnamon, mint
For Health	Avocado, black bean, cinnamon, citrus, cloves, dandelion, dyer's chamomile, echinacea, elder tree berries, spinach, strawberry, thyme
For Insight	Citrus, holy basil, marjoram, mugwort, poppy, yarrow
For Love	Beet, blackberry, caraway, carrot, cherry, cinnamon, cloves, cranberry, hawthorn, hibiscus, lavender, lemon balm, plum, prickly pear/nopal, rhubarb, rose
For Luck	Aloe, chili pepper, citrus, comfrey, fennel, garlic, juniper, mint, thyme
For Money	Black tea (Earl Grey), bok choy, cinnamon, cloves, dill, loquat, mint, purple basil, wild buckwheat, wild ginger
For Peace	Annatto, dyer's chamomile, lavender, lemon balm, marjoram, passion flower fruit, sagebrush, sumac
For Protection	Chili pepper, cinnamon, citrus, cranberry, garlic, holy basil, marjoram, mint, turmeric, walnut
For Success	Apricot, blackberry, celery, marjoram, rosemary
For Travel	Caraway, fennel, rosemary, star anise
For Wisdom	Dyer's chamomile, holy basil, juniper, marjoram, mugwort, peach, sagebrush, thyme, yarrow

Colors

For selecting specific colors to add powers to your spells, refer to page 163.

Additional Ways to Enhance Plants

Water Submersion

Plants can be added to magical waters like rose water and moon water to strengthen and shift their properties.

Charging Plants

Some practitioners recommend *charging* plants to be used in kitchen spells, whether that means including them as ingredients for meals or employing them for other kinds of magic such as carrying, burying, or offering. Charging the plants harnesses the power of our awareness.

Hold the plant in your hands and concentrate, pushing your intention through your palms into the plant.

See what the plant communicates back:

Is it saying *yes* or *no*? Trust your intuition to feel the response.

If the answer is *yes*, breathe deeply and focus on your intention, tensing before you exhale to send energy to your palms. Repeat four times more. The plant material is charged with a different aspect of the spell with each breath, corresponding to the five elements.

If the answer is *no*, breathe deeply and slowly five times. Direction on what path to take forward will appear in your mind.

Regardless of the answer, take a moment to express gratitude to the plant and our ancestors for bringing us together.

Poultices

Poultices are for topical healing by packing herbs onto an affected area of the skin. They are traditionally used to treat rashes, stings, bites, blemishes, sore muscles, and other irritations. To make a poultice, gather the herbs you wish to use and crush them with a mortar and pestle or food processor. Add two tablespoons of hot water. Traditionally, one would use clay powder or baking soda to bind the poultice. I like making poultices with calming ground oatmeal and a pH-balancing dash of apple cider vinegar for skin irritations. For soreness, I make them with muscle-soothing Epsom salts. Add your chosen binding material slowly, teaspoon by teaspoon, until the poultice has thickened and holds together enough to be applied to the affected area. Use a gentle gauze or cheesecloth wrapping to keep it in place.

Tinctures

Tinctures are concentrated extractions of plant oils used. They are created by soaking plant matter in strong alcohol. The alcohol draws out the plant's oils and medicinal properties. Brandy is preferable, but vodka or anything 80-proof will work. (For children, make with apple cider vinegar or vegetable glycerin—a by-product of handmade soap.) To make a tincture, chop or smash the plants. Loosely fill a jar with them and cover them with the alcohol. Seal and store in a cool, dark place for six weeks, shaking the jar every day for the first week. Then, strain the liquid and store it in a dark-colored glass bottle. This tincture will last five to ten years or more.

Essential Oils

Essential oils are collected by boiling plants and skimming the oil off the top of the water. Different oils are thought to treat a wide range of ailments when used topically.

There is a simpler, less punishing method to draw out the oils, though. Submerge plant cuttings in olive oil and leave them out in the sun. For example, fresh calendula petals submerged in olive oil can be put in a jar on a sunny windowsill for a month and stirred daily. The oil will be suffused with calendula oil. Strain, and store it in a cool, dark place. Calendula oil treats skin irritations.

Spells to Jump-Start Your Grimoire

Here are some starter spells to help you on your grimoire journey.

Air Spells

DANDELION MESSAGES

To send a message to a loved one, near or far, focus on what you need them to know and blow dandelion seeds in their direction.

HERBS IN THE WIND

Select sprigs of plants whose meanings and colors relate to something you long for. (See part two.) Find an open place atop a hill or mountain where trees, hills, or walls do not block the wind. Once you arrive and pause, thinking about your spell, one of your hands will tingle with magical electricity. Hold your herbs in this hand and visualize or speak your wish. First, face north. Take a breath and blow some of the leaves in that direction. Turn east and repeat, and again to the south. Facing west, blow all the remaining herbs from your hand. Raise your arms and breathe in, connecting upward to the fifth direction. Your needs will be met.

READ THE TREES

Choose a tree that calls to you, or whose meaning (see the Trees, Herbs, and Roots Grimoire) is related to a question you have. Focus on the movement of the branches in the wind as you ask the question in your mind. Slowly, you will start to read the tree's language, as if its twigs and branches were written letters. You will find clues to what is to come.

SEND POWER

To send your powers to help someone, select sprigs of plants whose meaning and colors relate to their needs. Go to a place of moving water, such as a lake, stream, river, or ocean. Hold the plants tightly in your power hand (the hand you do not write with). Visualize what is needed. With a sweeping motion, scatter the plants into the air over the water. The power has been sent.

Water Spells

TEA LEAVES

To read tea leaves, brew a cup with some type of loose-leaf tea, preferably one whose properties relate to your question or desire. (Please refer to part two to choose your leaves.) You may choose from the plants listed as safe for consumption, but to be sure you have a suitable variety, you can purchase them or grow your own. Examples from your garden could also include mint, chamomile, and lavender.

Consider what you would like to know as you drink. When you've finished drinking the liquid, quickly turn the cup upside down for a moment and then flip it back right side up. Look at the shape of the leaves. What do you see? Trust your intuition to tell you what the images created by the tea leaves mean.

WHO IS VISITING ME?

Sometimes, spirits come to help us. Focusing on these positive presences gives them power. To see who is visiting you, steep purple irises in hot water. Using paper or any surface that you feel drawn to, dip a paintbrush into the iris water and paint a pool of it into a shape that feels right. It will be light purple. Pick any purple ink or watercolor paint and add it to the pool. As the spell dries, the face of the visiting spirit will emerge.

POPPYSEED ANSWERS

If you wish to know the answer to a complex question, write it in blue ink on white paper. Wrap the paper into a cloth with a poppy seedpod. Place it beneath your pillow. You will dream the answer.

LOVE AND PEACE BATHS

To draw love to you, add rose water to your bath. To make rose water, soak rose petals in water, adding a whole clove to prevent molding. Or you can add petals directly to your bathwater. To cultivate peace, add sumac to the rose water. To enhance the spell, add Epsom salts, which will calm your nervous system and soothe sore muscles. Breathe deeply and visualize being surrounded by love and peace. **Note:** If you add salts, drink plenty of water.

Fire Spells

BASIL AND COALS

To forecast the success of a relationship, place two fresh basil leaves on a smoldering coal. If the leaves burn quietly to ashes, the relationship will be harmonious. If there is crackling, there will be arguments. Consider whether the relationship is unhealthy if the leaves crackle and burst apart.

CANDLES AND LEAVES

Cast a spell by selecting plants whose meanings and colors relate to your goals and desires. (Consult part two for plant meanings. Color meanings are listed on page 163.) Arrange the plants at the base of two candles. Light the candles and gaze into their flames, visualizing the outcome you desire.

SPELL FOR A HAPPY WINTER

When zinnias and goldenrod are both in bloom, cut a stem of a red or yellow zinnia and one of goldenrod. Tie them together and hang them upside down to dry in a dim, airy space. When they have dried, raise them toward the sun and say:

Flowers bright in soft sun,
protect me
from winter grief.
Shine in me
when summer
is gone.

When feeling wintery sadness, repeat:

Flowers bright in soft sun.

Crush the dry flowers and place them in an envelope. Keep them until the following summer solstice, when you should burn them in a ritual fire. Begin the cycle again in the early autumn when the zinnias and goldenrod are back in bloom.

HERBS AND FLAMES

To meet a need, select herbs whose meanings and powers relate to your wishes. Cut a piece of paper into a triangle and write or make a symbol of your need on the paper. Place the enchanted herbs in the center of the paper and fold the corners in, tucking the third corner under so it becomes a closed packet. Build a roaring fire. Throw the herb packet into the fire. As it first touches the flames, visualize your need until the fire consumes the packet.

TO DISAPPEAR

Place these items between two candles:

- Poppy seeds for invisibility
- Cloves for protection and to cause confusion
- Glass for transparency

Light the candles and focus on your wish, breathing eight times. Let the candle burn as you consider why you want to disappear. To seal the spell, say:

Ancestors, thank you.
I am grateful for my light.
I must have stealth
to gather strength
to build my bones
and cool my eyes
to heal my heart
and spread my wings.
Soon, I will shine.
Soon, I will fly.

Blow out the candle, envisioning what you wish to hide from. As you recover, you will be unnoticed.

Earth Spells

SOIL SPELL

Select plants whose meanings and colors relate to your desires. Place them in a cloth or paper bag and take them to a wild place. Dig a small hole in the ground with your hands and place them in it. As you concentrate intensely on your intention, cover the plants with soil. Rise and immediately leave the area.

Say, *It is done.*

EARTH BLOTS

If you are feeling unsettled, rub a handful of soil over a blank piece of paper. Ask the soil, "How can I find my footing?" Pour the soil off the paper and find the answer in the symbols left behind.

SOIL WRITING

Select a fallen stick from a tree whose meaning and magical properties relate to your intention. Find some soft soil at the base of the tree. Brush away any dry leaves and without disturbing any living ground cover, write your wish into the earth using your stick. Leave your stick with the writing and press your palms to the tree trunk. Let your intentions flow from your hands. When you feel ready, thank the tree for listening.

HOUSEPLANT GEOMANCY

A houseplant is the spell. Select a plant whose meaning and properties relate to your hopes for home and family. Care for the plant and speak to it about your wishes. Keep it in your home, remembering to pause, recognize, and thank it for its unique energy.

HEAL A WILTING PLANT

Place the plant in a pot with moon water, fresh soil, ground eggshells, and old leaves of the same plant. Speak this incantation to the plant each morning or evening: *Stay with me.* Add moon water when the plant is dry.

*Now that you have knowledge
of spellcraft and a connection
to the fifth direction,
your magic practice will bring
you joy and abundance.*

CONCLUSION: A BENEDICTION OF RUNES

Plant magic runs through your every cell.

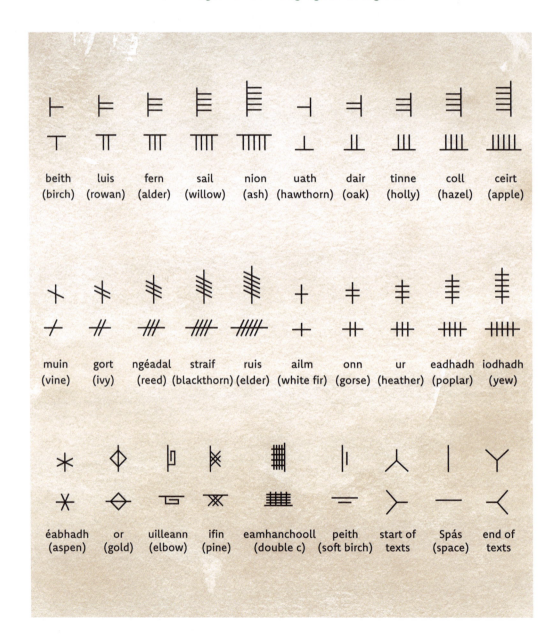

The ancient Irish runic language *Ogham* (Oh-wam) is a Pict language of tree symbols from northern Scotland preceding Gaelic. Each Ogham rune connects to a specific tree and honors the connections of all who are born of stardust. Please use this Benediction of Ogham Runes to remind yourself:

You are nature.
You are creative.
You are loved.
You are powerful.
You can be vulnerable.
You deserve joy.
You are beautiful.

Long ago, an ancient wind was born. It wasn't there, and then it was. It raced, gusting across the water, causing a storm to be born, too. And then, it died. More winds were born from the storm that it created. Your ancestor saw the storm and felt the rush of the ancient wind's children. Your ancestor drank from the water that the ancient storm's rains became. So did the ancestors of your plants.

Winds and waters have moved through time and all beings. We understand the beauty of plants because we share the same family. We all come from the same stars, winds, waters, and sunbeams. Plants remind us to celebrate the world's magic and to remember that we are all connected. We are all descended from the ancient wind.

Please accept this spell from our ancestors as a blessing whispered to you across time, over the winds.

Ogham Runes Spell

WIND WHISPERS OF YOU
(Breathe deeply)

*Under the winter's last moon
Your power gathers.
Speck of stardust, may you dance alive!
Awaken, limitless.*

*Morning mist, living waters shimmering
on the tiniest leaves.
May you sense the sunbeams
as if for the first time.*

*Cool bark against your cheek
safe and snug
May you stand tall and true.
Your fingertips graze the sky.*

*The willow weeps into the river.
The waters cheer her with sparkling sun.
May her roots weave happiness
into your heart's songs.*

*The dawn breaks with tender light.
Your song rings through the rocky valley*

Like a bright petal floating in the dark creek,
may your leaves delight in the wind, dancing.

When the dark sky sparkles cool,
may your flower be a firework
blossoming effortlessly.
Joyful, gentle your heart's petals open.

The midsummer moon
paints the treetops
with silver secrets.
May you scry the ancient whispers.

In the stark, rippling desert sun,
hidden waters rest.
May the remembered songs of nighttime's crickets soar
protected by your boundaries, strong as thorns.

A quick bird races
through clouds unbroken and low.
May you rest safe under Mother Earth's warmest blankets.
May you soak in her tender love.

Whisper this spell and know you are never alone. You are a child of the stars. Your family is all of creation.

BIBLIOGRAPHY

Adrosko, Rita J. *Natural Dyes and Home Dyeing.* New York: Dover, 1971.

Anonymous (authorship of 1833 ed. credited to Mrs. Rebecca He). *The Morals of Flowers.* London: Longman, Rees, Orme, Brown, Green & Longman, 1836. www.biodiversitylibrary.org/bibliography/159588.

Bearfoot, William. *Mother Nature's Dyes and Fibers.* New York: Scribner, 1975.

Behan, Babs, and Kim Lightbody. *Botanical Inks: Plant-to-Print Dyes, Techniques, and Projects.* London: Quadrille, 2019.

Booth, Abigail. *Wild Dyer: A Maker's Guide to Natural Dyes with Projects to Create and Stitch.* New York: PA Press, 2019.

Bradley, Milton. *Elementary Color.* Springfield, MA: Milton Bradley Co., 1895.

Buchanan, Rita. *A Dyer's Garden: From Plant to Pot, Growing Dyes for Natural Fibers.* Loveland, CO: Interweave Press, 1995.

Buchanan, Rita. *A Weaver's Garden: Growing Plants for Dyes and Natural Fibers.* Mineola, NY: Dover Publications, 1999.

Buen, Gina, and Marin Clark, eds. *The Botanical Mind: Art, Mysticism and the Cosmic Tree.* London: Camden Art Centre, 2020.

Burgess, Rita. *Harvesting Color: How to Find and Make Natural Dyes.* New York: Artisan, 2011.

Burton, Richard Francis. *The Ogham-Runes and El-Mushajjar: A Study.* London: Harrison & Sons, 1882. https://burtoniana.org/pamphlets/1882-The-Ogham-Runes-and-El-Mushajjar/index.html.

Chopra, Deepak, and Joan Borysenko. *Pathways to God.* Carlsbad, CA: Hay House, 2000.

Codex Azcatitlan. N.p., 1530. PDF retrieved from the Library of Congress, www.loc.gov/item/2021668122.

Culpeper, Nicholas, and Steven Foster. *Culpeper's Complete Herbal* (originally published 1653). Illustrated and annotated edition. New York: Sterling Publishing Company, 2019.

Cummings, E. E. Edited by George James Firmage. *Complete Poems, 1904–1962.* New York: Liveright, 1994.

Cunningham, Scott. *Cunningham's Encyclopedia of Magical Herbs.* St. Paul, MN: Llewellyn Publications, 1985.

Cunningham, Scott. *Magical Herbalism: The Secret Craft of the Wise.* Woodbury, MN: Llewellyn, 2021.

Dean, Jenny, and Karen Diadick Casselman. *Wild Color: The Complete Guide to Making and Using Natural Dyes.* New York: Potter Craft, 2010.

De Bingen, Hildegard. *The Book of Divine Works.* N.p., 1210–30. PDF retrieved from the Library of Congress, www.loc.gov/item/2021668244.

Denisse, Etienne. *Flore d'Amérique, dessinée d'après nature sur les lieux. Riche collection de plantes les plus remarquables, fleurs & fruits de grosseur & de grandeur naturelle.* Paris: Gihaut, 1847. www.biodiversitylibrary.org/item/185335.

Duerr, Sasha. *Natural Palettes: Inspiration from Plant-Based Color.* New York: PA Press, 2020.

Duerr, Sasha, and Ava Brackaett. *Natural Color: Vibrant Plant Dye Projects for Your Home and Wardrobe.* Berkeley, CA: Watson-Guptill Publications, 2016.

Everett, Nicholas. *Alphabet of Galen: Pharmacy from Antiquity to the Middle Ages: A Critical Edition of the Latin Text with English Translation and Commentary* (originally published 127–219 CE). University of Toronto Press, 2012.

Greenaway, Kate, and Jean Marsh. *The Illuminated Language of Flowers* (originally published 1884). New York: Henry Holt & Co., 1978.

Grieve, M. (Maud). *A Modern Herbal: The Medicinal, Culinary, Cosmetic, and Economic Properties, Cultivation, and Folk-Lore of Herbs, Grasses, Fungi, Shrubs, & Trees with All Their Modern Scientific Uses.* New York: Harcourt, Brace & Company, 1931.

Herbal. Lombardi, North Italy via the British Library. Compiled by the Palatino Press. (Originally published 1440.)

Hernandez, Francisco. *Rerum medicarum Novae Hispaniae thesaurus, seu, Plantarum animalium mineralium Mexicanorum historia.* Romae, Ex typographeio Vitalis Mascardi, 1651. www.biodiversitylibrary.org/bibliography/53514.

Just, Ernest Everett. *The Biology of the Cell Surface.* Philadelphia: P. Blakiston's Son and Co., 1939. www.biodiversitylibrary.org/item/28768.

Khandekar, Narayan, et al. *An Atlas of Rare and Familiar Colour: The Harvard Museum's Forbes Print Collection.* Los Angeles: Atelier Editions, 2019.

Kimmerer, Robin Wall. *Braiding Sweetgrass.* Minneapolis: Milkweed Editions, 2015.

Kynes, Sandra. *Plant Magic: A Year of Green Wisdom for Pagans.* Woodbury, MN: Llewlyn, 2017.

Lamb, Hannah. *Poetic Cloth: Creating Meaning in Textile Art.* London: Batsford, 2019.

Largo, Michael. *The Big, Bad Book of Botany: The World's Most Fascinating Flora.* New York: HarperCollins, 2019.

Laws, Bill. *Fifty Plants That Changed the Course of History.* Buffalo, NY: Firefly Books, 2021.

Lee, David. *Nature's Palette: The Science of Plant Color.* University of Chicago Press, 2010.

Logan, Jason. *Make Ink: A Forager's Guide to Natural Ink Making.* New York: Abrams, 2018.

Magnus, Saint Albertus. *The Book of Secrets of Albertus Magnus: Of the Virtues of Herbs, Stones, and Certain Beasts.* Translated by Michael R. Best and Frank Brightman.Oxford University Press, 1974. Accessed from the Library of Congress. www.loc.gov/item/75287558.

Marks, Diana F., and Donna Farrell. *Glues, Brews, and Goos: Recipes and Formulas for Almost Any Classroom Project.* Vol 2. Westport, CT: Teacher Ideas Press, 2003.

Maund, B., et al. *The Botanist: containing accurately coloured figures of tender and hardy ornamental plants; with descriptions, scientific and popular; intended to convey both moral and intellectual gratification.* London: R. Groombridge, 1842. www.biodiversitylibrary.org/item/99820.

McLaughlin, Chris. *A Garden to Dye For: How to Use Plants from the Garden to Create Natural Colors for Fabrics and Flyers.* Pittsburgh: St. Lynn's Press, 2014.

Midrash, Bereshit Rabbah 10, The Sefaria Midrash Rabbah, 2022.

Milton, John. *Paradise Lost* (originally published in 1667). New York: Penguin Classics, 2003.

Monardes, Nicolás, et al. *Ioyfullnewes out of the new-found uuorlde: wherein are declared, the rare and singuler vertues of diuers herbs, trees, plantes, oyles & stones, with their applications, as well to the use of physique as of chirurgery ... Also the portrature of the said hearbs.* London: Printed by E. Allde, by the assignee of Bonham Norton, 1596. www.biodiversitylibrary.org/item/31924.

Neddo, Nick. *The Organic Artist.* Beverly, MA: Quarry Books, 2015.

Noyes Vanderpoll, Emily. *Color Problems: A Practical Manual for the Lay Student of Color.* New York: Longmans, Green, 1903.

O'Donohue, John. *To Bless the Space between Us: A Book of Blessings.* New York: Doubleday, 2008.

Ridgeway, Robert. *Color Standards and Color Nomenclature.* Washington, D.C.: Ridgeway, 1912.

St. Clair, Kassia. *Secret Lives of Color.* New York: Penguin, 2017.

Schetky, Ethel Jane McD., ed. *Dye Plants and Dyeing—A Handbook.* Brooklyn Botanic Garden, 1964.

Shakespeare, William. *Macbeth* (originally published in 1623). Ware, Hertsfordshire: Wordsworth Editions, 1992.

Shakespeare, William. *The Tragedy of Hamlet, Prince of Denmark* (originally published in 1603). London: Folio Society, 1954.

Simard, S. *Finding the Mother Tree: Discovering the Wisdom of the Forest.* New York: Alfred A. Knopf, 2021.

Steinbeck, John. *Travels with Charley: In Search of America.* New York: Viking Press, 1962.

Syme, Patrick. *Wermer's Nomenclature of Colours—Adapted to Zoology, Botany, Chemistry, Mineralogy, Anatomy, and the Arts.* Edinburgh: Art Meets Science, 1814.

Taylor, J. E. *The Sagacity & Morality of Plants: A Sketch of the Life & Conduct of the Vegetable Kingdom.* London: Chatto and Windus, 1884. www.biodiversitylibrary.org/item/45989.

Vienna Color Cabinet. Vienna/Prague: Im Verlage der v. Schönfeldschen Handlung, 1794.

von Goethe, Johann Wolfgang. *Theory of Colours* (originally published in 1810). Republished by MIT Press, 1970.

Waller, Richard. *Table of Physiological Colors Both Mixt and Simple.* Philosophical Transactions of the Royal Society of London, 1686.

Wiener Farbenkabinet: Oder, vollständiges Musterbuch aller Natur Grund und Zusammensetzungsfarben, Vienna/Prague: Im Verlage der v. Schönfeldschen Handlung, 1794. https://archive.org/details/WienerFarbenkab00.

Wilkins, Marylin. *California Dye Plants.* Santa Rosa, CA: Thresh Publications, 1976.

ACKNOWLEDGMENTS

Thank you to my brilliant editor, Maria Lourdes Riillo, for her vision and discernment. To illustrator Claire Harrup, I love your beautiful work; thank you! Thank you to the Running Press team, including Leah Gordon and Susan Van Horn. You make gorgeous books. Ashley Benning, thank you for your outstanding copyediting. Thank you to the NIH-SEPA ESTA Grant team, especially Corin Slown, for all your support and encouragement; I have loved the years-long botanical conversation with Irene Tsatsos, Sean Lehmayer, and my fellow researchers on the Getty PST From the Ground Up team. I learned so much from you all—thank you.

I am so grateful to the Cal State Monterey Bay Library team for tracking down all the weird and obscure old books I requested and to the Marina, CA, community for all your kind support and inspiring passion for nature at home. Thank you to Kathleen Founds for toasting every step of this process. I'm super glad we switched from cheap champagne to kombucha.

I consider my unstoppable agent, Liz Nealon, part of my foraged family. Thank you, Liz, for being my dream-come-true mentor. Thank you to my husband for his patience with the mysterious jars I leave all over our counter, table, garden, and windowsills. To my children, thank you for sharing flowers, leaves, and acorns with me and always inspiring me. You fill my life with joy.

INDEX

air element, 122, 124-125, 164-165, 177, 181-182
air spells, 164-165, 177, 181-182
ancient manifesting spell, 154
annual plants, 13-14, 30-31, 56, 66
Art Wound, 157-160
arts projects, 166-173
astrology, 68-71

bath salts, 172-173, 180, 183
beauty spell, 36
Benediction of Ogham Runes, 189-191
biological crusts, 4-5
birth signs, 68-69
blessings, 97, 166, 172-173, 189

calendars, 70-71, 166-173
caution, exercising, 5
Celtic tree astrology, 68-71
chakras
    crown chakra, 165
    heart chakra, 165
    locations of, 164-165
    navel chakra, 165
    pelvic chakra, 165
    root chakra, 159, 164
    sacral chakra, 63, 165
    solar plexus chakra, 159
    third-eye chakra, 85, 165
    throat chakra, 165
color baths, 42, 119, 125-136, 142-143, 150, 166
color extraction
    dry pigments, 125, 133-135
    elements and, 40, 122-134
    for flowers, 43-66
    freezing process, 40, 122-125, 131
    for fruits, 99-119
    hapa zome technique, 18, 40, 123-124, 166-168
    heating process, 122, 132
    for herbs, 72-94
    for inks, 135-142
    for paints, 135, 143-154
    process of, 40, 122-134
    for roots, 72-94
    soaking process, 18, 122, 125-136
    steam eco-printing, 40, 125
    for trees, 72-94
    for vegetables, 99-119
color magic, 19, 31, 155-162
Color Magic Cards, 161-162
color theory, 155-157
color wheel, 156-160
color wheel healing spell, 158-160
colors
    breathing, 164-165
    color extraction process, 40, 122-134
    emotions and, 156, 160-163
    of flowers, 43-66
    foraging and, 160
    of fruits, 99-119
    of herbs, 72-94
    language of, 20, 96, 157-160
    meanings of, 163
    of roots, 72-94
    of trees, 72-94
    of vegetables, 99-119
companion plantings, 22-26
companionship spell, 26
compost, 98
crystal balls, 2, 40
crystals, 68-69

daytime gardens, 16-17
dream garden, 11-12
dream spell, 12

earth element, 122-123, 162, 164, 177, 186
earth spells, 162, 177, 186
egg dyes, 169-171
egg tempera, 143-144, 158
elements

198

air element, 122, 124-125, 164-165, 177, 181-182
air spells, 164-165, 177, 181-182
color extraction and, 40, 122-134
earth element, 122-123, 162, 164, 177, 186
earth spells, 162, 177, 186
fifth element, 97, 116, 165
fire element, 122, 125, 159, 165, 177, 184-185
fire spells, 177, 184-185
harnessing, 40, 122-134
reaping plants and, 121-187
spells and, 151-154, 158-162, 164-165, 174-179, 181-186
water element, 122-126, 151-154, 158-162, 165, 177, 179, 182-183, 186
water spells, 151-154, 158-162, 179, 182-183, 186
encaustic paints, 147-148
essential oils, making, 181

fifth direction, 181, 187
fifth element, 97, 116, 165
finger paint, 148
fire element, 122, 125, 159, 165, 177, 184-185
fire spells, 177, 184-185
flames, reading, 2, 40, 184-185
flowers
　annuals, 13-14, 30-31, 56, 66
　carrying, 42
　catalog of, 43-66
　colors of, 43-66
　essence of, 42
　extracting color from, 43-66
　grimoire for, 40-66
　harvesting, 40-66
　healing properties of, 43-66
　language of, 41, 74, 90, 103
　magic of, 41-66
　meanings of, 43-66
　names of, 43-66
　perennials, 13, 30-31, 47-48, 56
　sleeping with, 42

　traditional uses of, 43-66
　wearing, 42
foraging
　basics of, 6-7
　colors and, 160
　for gardens, 27
　places for, 7
　for plants, 1-8
　prohibited areas, 7
　reasons for, 6
　scenery and, 7
　scrying methods, 2-8
　spell for, 8
　supplies for, 6
　techniques for, 7
foraging spell, 8
Four Sisters, 23
frozen baths, 40, 131
fruits
　catalog of, 99-119
　colors of, 99-119
　extracting color from, 99-119
　harvesting, 99-119
　healing properties of, 99-119
　magic of, 99-119
　meanings of, 99-119
　names of, 99-119
　traditional uses of, 99-119

garden design, 27-32
gardens
　beauty spell, 36
　companion plantings, 22-26
　companionship spell, 26
　daytime gardens, 16-17
　designing, 27-32
　dream garden, 11-12
　dream spell, 12
　foraging for, 27
　healing garden, 16-18, 24
　Hecate's garden, 15
　laying out, 27-32
　light spell, 17
　magical gardens, 9-36
　measuring, 31

INDEX

moon gardens, 9-14, 29
moon phase gardening, 13-14
moon shadows in, 14-15
planning, 27-32
plant arrangements in, 31-32
planting zones for, 21-22, 31
pollinator gardens, 20-22
pollinators for, 9-10, 14, 20-22, 157
protecting, 32-34
rainbow pigment garden, 19
saving seeds from, 7, 21, 32
scrying and, 27-28
shadows in, 14-17
shadows spell, 15
for shady areas, 28, 30-31
soil for, 26-27
spell cloths, 18, 84
for sunny areas, 16, 19, 28, 30-31
urban gardens, 28, 33
gathering plants
  caution with, 5
  for companion plantings, 22-26
  foraging and, 1-8
  for magical gardens, 9-36
  scrying and, 2-8
  tips for, 1-36
  see also plants
gemstones, 68-69
gouache paintings, 146-147
gratitude, expressing, 8, 97, 179, 185
grimoires
  creating, 174-187
  explanation of, 39-41
  flower grimoire, 40-66
  for harvesting plants, 39-119
  herb grimoire, 67-94
  jump-starting, 181-186
  kitchen grimoire, 95-119
  as record of plants, 39-114
  root grimoire, 67-94
  as spell book, 39-41
  spells for, 181-186
  tree grimoire, 67-94

harvest
  flower grimoire for, 40-66
  of flowers, 40-66
  of fruits, 99-119
  grimoires for, 39-119
  herb grimoire for, 67-94
  of herbs, 67-94
  kitchen grimoire for, 95-119
  root grimoire for, 67-94
  tree grimoire for, 67-94
  of vegetables, 99-119
  see also plants
healing garden, 16-18, 24. *See also* gardens
healing properties
  of flowers, 43-66
  of fruits, 99-119
  of herbs, 72-94
  of plants, 16-17, 24, 34-35, 43-119
  of roots, 72-94
  of trees, 72-94
  of vegetables, 99-119
healing spells, 158-160, 186
herbs
  bundles of, 168-169
  catalog of, 72-94
  colors of, 72-94
  companion plantings, 24-25
  extracting color from, 72-94
  grimoire for, 67-94
  harvesting, 67-94
  healing properties of, 72-94
  magic of, 72-94
  meanings of, 72-94
  names of, 72-94
  traditional uses of, 72-94
hexes, 76, 88, 108

ink
  acorn cap ink, 137
  berry ink, 142
  buckthorn berry ink, 138
  iron liquor, 136
  making, 135-142
  oak gall ink, 139

pokeberry ink, 140
walnut hull ink, 141
ink divination spell, 153-154
insecticides, 34
insects, 24-25, 34
intentions, setting, 175-177
invasive plants, 5-7, 19, 83, 94

journals, 15, 41, 166-167. *See also* grimoires

kitchen grimoire, 95-119
kitchen scraps, 98

layered letters spell, 154
lichens, 4
light spell, 17
love baths, 183
love spells, 46, 52, 56, 60, 94, 115

magic
   book of, 39, 174-177
   color magic, 19, 31, 155-162
   of flowers, 41-66
   forms of, 41, 179
   of fruits, 99-119
   Green Magic, 39, 121, 174
   of herbs, 72-94
   kitchen magic, 95-119
   of roots, 72-94
   spells and, 174-187
   of trees, 72-94
   of vegetables, 99-119
magic practice, developing, 39-119, 121-191
magical gardens, 9-36. *See also* gardens
magical plants, 1-36, 39-119, 121-191. *See also* plants
magical relationships, 96-97
manifestation, 39, 46, 154, 162, 167, 175
mantras, 15, 17, 36
meals, 23, 95-97
meditative spells, 8, 150, 162

milk paint, 149
moon gardens, 9-14, 29
moon phases, 13-14
moon shadows, 14-15
moon water, 13, 153, 179, 186
mosses, 4-5

Ogham runes, 189-191
Otherworld
   communication with, 15, 20, 153
   connecting with, 68, 71, 93, 137, 150-154, 166-167
   threats from, 102
   wisdom from, 163

paint
   edible paint, 148-149
   egg tempera, 143-144, 158
   encaustic paint, 147-148
   finger paint, 148
   gouache paint, 146-147
   making, 135, 143-154
   milk paint, 149
   puffy paint, 150
   watercolor paint, 144-152, 158-160
paintings, 143-154, 158-162
paintings spells, 151-152, 158-162
peace baths, 183
perennial plants, 13, 30-31, 47-48, 56
pesticides, 20-21, 24
pests, 20-25
pigments, dry, 125
plant bundles, 125, 168-169
plant-based diets, 23, 95-97
planting zones, 21-22, 31
plants
   annuals, 13-14, 30-31, 56, 66
   arranging in garden, 31-32
   bundling, 125, 168-169
   catalog of, 43-66, 72-94, 99-119
   caution with, 5
   charging, 179
   disturbing, 4-7, 186
   enhancing, 179-181
   flower grimoire for, 40-66

201

foraging for, 1-8
gathering, 1-36
grimoires for, 39-114
growing without seeds, 33-36
harvesting, 39-119
healing properties of, 16-17, 24, 34-35, 43-119
herb grimoire for, 67-94
invasive plants, 5-7, 19, 83, 94
kitchen grimoire for, 95-119
magical plants, 1-36, 39-119, 121-191
meanings of, 43-66, 72-94, 99-119, 178
mystery of, 166-167
perennials, 13, 30-31, 47-48, 56
planting zones for, 21-22, 31
pollinators for, 9-10, 14, 20-22, 157
reaping, 121-187
record of, 39-114
root grimoire for, 67-94
runes and, 188-191
saving seeds from, 7, 21, 32
for shade, 28, 30-31
for sun, 16, 19, 28, 30-31
tree grimoire for, 67-94
see also specific types
pollinator gardens, 20-22
pollinators, 9-10, 14, 20-22, 157
poultices, making, 179-180
puffy paint, 150

rainbow pigment garden, 19
reaping plants
arts projects, 166-173
color baths, 42, 119, 125-136, 142-143, 150, 166
color extraction process, 40, 122-134
color magic, 19, 31, 155-162
creating grimoire and, 174-187
dry pigments, 125, 133-135
elements and, 121-187
enhancing plants, 179-181
making inks, 135-142

making paints, 135, 143-154
spells and, 174-179, 181-186
see also plants
relationships, magical, 96-97
rituals, 41, 163, 174-177, 184
roots
catalog of, 72-94
colors of, 72-94
extracting color from, 72-94
grimoire for, 67-94
healing properties of, 72-94
magic of, 72-94
meanings of, 72-94
names of, 72-94
traditional uses of, 72-94
rose curtains, 125, 168-169
runes, benediction of, 188-191
runes spell, 190-191

salt baths, 172-173, 180, 183
scrapbooks, 166-167
scrying
art of, 2-8
developing ability of, 2-8, 40, 71
explanation of, 2-3
for foraging, 2-8
of gardens, 27-28
of humans, 40
methods of, 2-8
of trees, 72
of world, 174
seasonal arts projects, 166-173
seasonal calendars, 70-71, 166-173
seeds, growing without, 33-36
seeds, saving, 7, 21, 32
shadows, 14-17, 71, 75, 166
shadows spell, 15
soil, nourishing, 26-27
soil spells, 186
spell books, 39-41. *See also* grimoires
spell cloths, 18, 84
spells
air spells, 164-165, 177, 181-182
ancient manifesting spell, 154
beauty spell, 36

color cards for, 161-162
color wheel healing spell, 158-160
companionship spell, 26
constructing, 174-179
dream spell, 12
earth spells, 162, 177, 186
elements and, 151-154, 158-162, 164-165, 174-179, 181-186
fire spells, 177, 184-185
foraging spell, 8
for grimoires, 181-186
healing spells, 158-160, 186
hex spells, 108
ink divination spell, 153-154
layered letters spell, 154
light spell, 17
love spells, 46, 52, 56, 60, 94, 115
magic and, 174-187
meditative spells, 8, 150, 162
paintings spells, 151-152, 158-162
rituals and, 163, 174-177
runes spell, 190-191
shadows spell, 15
soil spells, 186
spell cloths, 18, 84
walking spell, 8
water spells, 151-154, 158-162, 179, 182-183, 186
winter spell, 184
summer solstice, 172, 184
sun baths, 56, 73, 85, 132
symbols, 14, 144, 153, 169, 185-186, 188-191

tea leaves, 2, 102, 182
Three Sisters, 23, 53
tinctures, making, 180
trees
    calendars and, 70-71
    catalog of, 72-94
    colors of, 72-94
    extracting color from, 72-94
    grimoire for, 67-94
    healing properties of, 72-94
    heart of, 72
    language of, 182, 189
    magic of, 72-94
    meanings of, 72-94
    names of, 72-94
    reading, 182
    scrying, 72
    symbols of, 189
    traditional uses of, 72-94

urban gardens, 28, 33

vegetables
    catalog of, 99-119
    colors of, 99-119
    extracting color from, 99-119
    harvesting, 99-119
    healing properties of, 99-119
    magic of, 99-119
    meanings of, 99-119
    names of, 99-119
    traditional uses of, 99-119

walking spell, 8
water element, 122-126, 151-154, 158-162, 165, 177, 179, 182-183, 186
water spells, 151-154, 158-162, 179, 182-183, 186
watercolor paint, 144-152, 158-160
Wheel of the Year, 70-71
winter solstice, 125, 168
winter spell, 184

ABOUT THE AUTHOR

ENID BAXTER RYCE is an author, artist, and filmmaker. Her books include *The Borderlands Tarot/El Tarot del Tierras Fronterizas* (Running Press, 2024). Enid exhibits her artworks internationally at museums and festivals. She makes natural art supplies as part of her five-year National Institutes of Health grant and botanical art as a researcher on a Getty Foundation PST Project for the Armory Center for the Arts. Part of this work was done with the Huntington Botanical Gardens. Enid has won awards for her work as an artist and arts educator. She lives with her family in Marina, California.